(justitia negavit)

Justice Denied

A Report How Justice Was Denied

By Mr. Peter Millman a

Government Inspector Appointed by DEFRA

When Presiding Over

A Non-Statutory Public Enquiry

In Bedfordshire. Ref. FPS/P0240/14A/1

Held 15th, 16th, 17th, September 2015

By Alan Bowers

Published by New Generation Publishing in 2020

First Edition

ISBN 978-1-80031-552-5

www.newgeneration-publishing.com

New Generation Publishing

CONTENTS IN "JUSTICE DENIED"

PREFACE

A Non-Statutory appeal under Wildlife and Countryside Act 1981 Section 53 -Schedule 14(4)(1). Public Inquiry. Ref. No. FPS/P0240/14A/1 was held in Bedfordshire September 2015.

The Inquiry was conducted by Mr. Peter Millman a Government Inspector appointed by DEFRA.

The appeal was against the decision of Central Bedfordshire Council not to make an order under Section53 (2) of The Wildlife and Countryside Act 1981.

At the beginning of the Inquiry Mr.Millman informed all who attended, that he would not permit Mr. Alan Bowers (Principle objector) to read his opening statement or his witness statement, (**because it was too long and most of its contents was irrelevant to the case.**) There were many objections to the Inspectors statement. However, he insisted that the Opening and Witness statements of Mr. Bowers could not be read out to the members of the public attending the Inquiry. The Inspector had been in possession of the statements long before the Inquiry. The Inspector stated that he and the Council had seen the statements and he therefore considered them as read.

The Inspector also banned Mr. Connaughton from reading out his statement and questioning certain Council Officials.

I contacted "JustAnswer" on the internet, explaining my situation regarding the Inspector refusing to allow me to read my statement at the Public Inquiry September 2015. I received the following statement from "Buachaill Solicitor".

"Failing to allow you to present your opening statement and witness statement is grounds to judicially review the decision made by the Inquiry as you were not allowed fair procedures in accordance with the Human Rights Act and Article 6 of the European Convention on Human Rights. The Inquiry can validly, exclude evidence and rule 10 gives them this power. However, they cannot exclude the evidence of the party affected by the right of way. This gives rise to a judicial review as it does not accord with the guarantee of fair procedures in decision making. You have the right to be heard and it has been violated here"

This document contains copies of Mr. Bowers statements.

After reading the statements, it is obvious why the Inspector did not wish the statements to be heard by the public attending the Inquiry. The statements reveal much information which would be detriment to the decision made by Central Bedfordshire Council.

The Inspector (Peter Millman) therefore denied me JUSTICE by not allowing me to inform the general public attending the true facts of the case, he also prevented Mr. Connaughton from informing those attending of other facts, and prevented him from questioning Council Officials which would also have been detrimental to the Councils case.

OPENING STATEMENT

AND

WITNESS STATEMENT

BY

ALAN BOWERS,

123b CLOPHILL Rd. MAULDEN, BEDS. MK45 2AE

Tel. 01525 860036   E.mail: bowers-alan@sky.com

To be presented

SECTION 53 WILDLIFE & COUNTRYSIDE ACT 1981

SCHEDULE 14 APPEAL, NON- STATUTORY

3 DAY   PUBLIC INQUIRY

15th, 16th, 17th, SEPTEMBER 2015

10 minutes.

WILDLIFE AND COUNTRYSIDE ACT 1981
SECTION 53 – SCHEDULE 14(4)(1) APPEAL
Reference: FPS/P0240/14A/1

OPENING STATEMENT by MR. ALAN BOWERS

HOW WE ARRIVED!

The reason for this Public Inquiry is long and controversial.

At a meeting, with Beds. County Council officers 21st. August 2008. I was advised by the officers to apply to the council to Delete Footpath 28, using Section 53 of The Wildlife and Countryside Act 1981 because the path was added to the definitive map using unreliable and questionable evidence 19th. July 1995. This was in addition to the two applications already submitted in 2004 to Extinguish the path using Section 118 of The Highways Act. and to Stop Up the path using Section 116 of the Highways Act.

My agent Jan Molyneaux submitted my application on 6th. October 2008 with following information, 23rd. March 2009 acknowledge by Mr. Maciejewski 6th. April 2009.

Note! Beds. County Council was disbanded March 2009 and replaced by Central Beds. Council.

Despite many requests made to Central Beds. Council, to process the applications; they were always reluctant to do so.

After seeking advice and persistent correspondence, they eventually agreed to meet to discuss the situation on 14th. December 2011. The meeting was attended by Mr. Maciejewski and a lady called Gema Harrison. I was accompanied by Councillor, Mr. Howard Lockey. After much debate, Mr. Maciejewski assured me that he would look at the applications in an impartial manner and with a fresh approach.

....

At a meeting, of the "Development Management Committee" of Central Bedfordshire Council on 13th. February 2013. The elected members of the committee were asked to consider all three applications, including the application made in 2008/9 under the "Wildlife and Countryside Act 1981. To delete footpath 28 Maulden Beds. The members approved two of the application, but rejected the Section 53 application.

The reason Section 53 application was rejected by the Elected Members was, because the members were not made aware of all evidence contained in the Council files at that time.

....

There followed many weeks of correspondence and discussion concerning the decision made by the committee, and the conduct and actions of certain officers. The Chief Executive and Chief Legal Advisor of the Council refused to answer many questions asked by myself and others. Eventually the council declared me VEXATIOUS and have stated they will not respond to any communication concerning Footpath28, from myself or my supporters.

Because of the rejection of my application, I made a Schedule 14 4(1) appeal to the Inspectorate 30th. April 2013, informing CBC at the same time. The appeal was considered by Inspector Mark Yates who dismissed the appeal 20th. September 2013. I applied for a Judicial Review of the case. December 2013. The decision made by Mark Yates was QUASHED by the court (and I was awarded costs). I was informed by the Treasurer Solicitor that because the decision had been Quashed, another Inspector would be designated to review the appeal.

I was informed by the Inspectorate 16th. June 2014 that a 2-day Public Inquiry would take place 3rd. December 2014. I was later informed by E.mail. 19th. June 2014 that the date of 3rd. December had been withdrawn, (No explanation was given).

I received a letter from the Inspectorate 30th.July 2014 that a 2-day Public Inquiry would take place 21st. January 2015 (the letter was written to Mr. Maciejewski but addressed to me. I contacted the Inspectorate to advise them of their mistake. The Inspectorate apologised and sent me the correct letter advising me of the details of the proposed date of the Inquiry 21st. January 2015 and also informed me that the Inspector attending the inquiry would be Alison Lea.

I was again informed by Ms. Baylis (Inspectorate) Wednesday 19th. August 2014; giving details of the proposed Public Inquiry, and the venue. I was informed that the Inquiry would be held Wednesday 21st. January 2015 at Beadlow Manor and was scheduled for 2 days.

I received an E.mail at 16.30 Friday 16th January 2015 informing me that the Inquiry due to be held 21st. January 2015 had been cancelled because of personal circumstances.

Leaving me, 2 working days; to alter all the arrangements which had been made. I contacted the Inspectorate on the morning of 19th. January 2015 (First available time) for more information and was told it was confidential.

I contacted the Inspectorate again in the morning of 11th. February 2015 and was again told that I could not be informed further. I was contacted by the Inspectorate by E.mail. at 12.48, 11th. February 2015, informing me that a new Inquiry would be arranged for mid-September 2015. (No other details).

I received a letter from Inspectorate, 20th. March 2015, informing me that a 3-day Inquiry would take place 15th. September 2015. I received another letter from the Inspectorate 22nd June 2015 informing me that for personal reasons Alison Lea would be replaced by Inspector Peter Millman.

I contacted the Inspectorate 29th. June 2015, requesting the reasons for the change of Inspector and was informed that for personal reasons Alison Lea would be taking extended leave. No other reason was given.

CONCLUSION!

I believe the Council and Inspectorate have been unhelpful and evasive leading up to this Public Inquiry.

I consider that the information I was given in January and June are excuses not reasons.

These are the events leading up to the present time and why we are here today.

For these reasons and others which will be explained in my witness statement later; this Inquiry has been shrouded in Mistrust, by me and many others.

Alan Bowers

1 hr. 20mins.

WITNESS STATEMENT PRESENTED TO
SCHEDULE 14 APPEAL
NON-STATUTORY INQUIRY 21ST- 22ND JANUARY
2015

SECTION 53 WILDLIFE & COUNTRYSIDE ACT
1981

Summary of Events, relating to the Unjustifiable adding
of Footpath 28
to the Rights of Way Definitive Map.

NOTE!
**All appendixes referred to in Statement are contained in
separate file.**

1) My name is Alan Bowers. I am 75 years old and have been
fighting to protect my property for over 20 years. I have
spent in excess of £110,000 and my family has had to
endure over 20 years of distress and financial burden. I
have suffered a nervous breakdown; my wife has also
received treatment for nerves, and I have acquired a
criminal record while trying to obtain justice. Of course,
our opponents (Local Authorities, user groups) are in a
different situation. Cost and time are not an issue to them!
It has been said by elected members of Local Authorities
"They are waiting for you to fall of your perch".

However, over these difficult years I have had the support
of other Authorities, including Police: Parish Council:
former Mid. Beds. District Council; and many ordinary
citizens. I have also received tremendous support from
Nadine Dorries MP

I am also aware of the same distress and financial burden being experienced by many other ordinary citizens regarding "Rights of Way" throughout the country.

I understand that this Non-Statutory Schedule 14 Inquiry is only the second one of its kind to be held in England. The first one took place in Somerset 28th October 2014.

That case, involving a very old brother and sister had been fought for over 43 years, and thanks to the skill and tireless determination of Marlene Masters a campaigner for justice regarding wrongfully imposed "Rights of Way" it appears that Justice may prevail.

During the many years I have been involved in this situation I have encountered a very convenient word, which has been used many times. The word is <u>Irrelevant</u> this word is used very often to prevent the truth being exposed.

I understand in law, all evidence relating to a specific case is <u>Relevant.</u>

2) In 1992, "Rights of Way Officers" of Beds. County Council (BCC) were approached by Mrs. H. Izzard of Maulden, Beds. concerning a path crossing my land.

She was encouraged by officers to apply to have the "Occupational Path" crossing the land to be classed as a Public Right of Way. Searches carried out by myself when I purchased the land revealed that the only Public Right of Way near the property was Bridleway 24 which ran parallel to the Occupational Path and arrived at the same point.
(Appendix 1)

Mrs. Izzard had already been informed in 1957 by the County Council Surveyor that the path in question was an Occupational Path and not a Public Right of Way. (Appendix 1a)

However, Mrs. Izzard was encouraged to obtain information from as many people as possible to support her application. Officers of BCC then proceeded to interview people suggested by Mrs. Izzard, most of whom were related in some way to her family. The Officers, (Particularly Zena Grant Collier) appeared over Zealous in their attempt to obtain information by writing to various people encouraging them to inform them of anyone they knew not related to Mrs. Izzard or Mrs. Huckle which could strengthen their case to Create Footpath 28. (Appendix 2) At no time during their investigation did the Officers interview me or previous owners of the land. I obtained Statutory Declarations from all the previous owners, who stated that the path had never been used by the public! One owner, Mr. Sharp had been the owner from 1946 until 1989. He was never approached by any investigating officers.

3) When the Agenda, which was produced by Mr. Glen Kilday (Directorate of Leisure Services) and supported by Mr. John Atkinson (Head of Legal & Member Services) was presented to the "Rights of Way Sub Committee" on 19th. July 1995, (Appendix 3) members were informed that there was no Documentary evidence to support the application, only User Evidence Forms obtained by the Officers. (No Statutory Declarations). The period to be considered to enforce (Section 31(1) of the Highways Act 1980) was 1936- 1956, (20-year period). Most of the User forms presented, relating to that period was from Friends

and Family of the Izzard family who owned the property up to 1946, and therefore could not be considered as members of the public. So, the period 1936-1946 should be disregarded! Indeed, there were no User forms presented by anyone living outside the Parish who could be considered as members of the public. The only Statutory Declarations were those of the owners.

4) The fact that this information was not made available to the members of the committee could be considered as deliberate in order to steer the members to a decision favoured by the Rights of Way Officers.

There was also a letter written to Mrs. Izzard in 1957 (Appendix 1) by the Authority at that time informing her that the pathway in question was not public but an occupational path. Although this was in the possession of the Rights of Way Officers at the time it was not made available to the Committee. Although the Officers informed the Committee that there was no documentary evidence to support the path being Public, there was evidence stating that the path was not Public. Failure to produce this document as evidence against the application can be considered as a deliberate act to steer the members to agreeing with the wishes of the Rights of Way Officers. The members therefore voted in favour of the application because they were not informed of all the facts. The Officers were under a Statutory Duty to make the Members aware of all evidence available to them at that time. Failure to inform the elected members of all the facts could be considered as a deliberate act to persuade them to agree to their wishes.

5) Sir Nicholas Lyell, Q, C, M.P. wrote a letter to Mr. Cleggett (Chief Executive of BCC) 9th. November 1995, enquiring about the Right of Way imposed upon my land.

The letter was answered by Mr Glen Kilday (Author of Agenda presented to BCC. committee 19th. July 1995). 29th. November 1995. Mr. Kilday informed Sir Nicholas Lyell that the path **"Was not recorded as a public right of way, this does not mean it was not a public right of way, only that it is not recorded as such"**. (Appendix 3)

6) In 1995. I obtained planning permission to build a house on the land which the disputed path ran. While the house was being constructed, I became aware of being observed by Rights of Way officers who drove away when they realised, they had been seen.

7) I arranged a meeting with the Chief Executive of BCC to take place 12 noon, 10th.October 1995, the purpose of the meeting was to ask why I was being observed by BCC officers. On arriving at the meeting, I was informed that the Chief Executive was not available, no reason was given. I was shown into a room where the officer who had been observing me;(Zena Grant Collier) was present with another officer Mr. Glen Kilday. (Who was the author of the report presented to the Committee in 1995). After a long discussion I was advised to apply to Mid. Beds. District Council to have the path extinguished using the Town & Country Planning Act because I had been granted planning permission to build my house. They also assured me that BCC would not object to the order.

8) I took their advice and applied to MBDC to have the path extinguished. I was informed by MBDC that they could not extinguish something that did not exist. At a meeting with BCC, 18th. December 1997, Mr. Glen Kilday informed me that if I agreed that the path existed, MBDC could extinguish it. I would not agree. I was informed that BCC would confirm that the path existed so that MBDC

could extinguish it. At the same meeting I asked the officers why they had changed the route of the path so that it passed through my new home. Mr. Kilday said to me the fact that the path passed through my house would give greater strength to the extinguishment. I was again informed that BCC would not object to the order to extinguish the path. This was also confirmed to MBDC. (Appendix 8). Mr. Glen Kilday informed me that in the event that the problem was not resolved, I should contact him and that they would remove the path using the Highways Act.

9) In a letter dated January 1996 by Zena Grant Collier (Definitive Map Modifications Officer). (Appendix 4) She states **"We do have evidence in our files that the path has been claimed as an "Occupational Path" (An Occupational Path cannot be a Public Path) and we have gathered evidence available, no matter which "Side" it takes to discover the truth".** No evidence was gathered from people who opposed the application.

10) It was at this time the Rights of Way Officers were prompted to contact various people who had supplied User Evidence Forms. In February 1997, Rights of Way officers wrote to various people to inform them that they would re-type their forms and visit them with a solicitor who would witness the signing of the forms, thereby making them Statutory Declarations. (Appendix 5). The solicitor's fees were paid by BCC. (Appendix 6).

11) In 1997 an order was issued by the Beds. County Council to add the path as a public Right of Way and was considered by an Inspector (Mr. R. Holley) appointed by the Secretary of State. He made a site visit. No public

Inquiry took place. He based his conclusion on written evidence supplied to him. (He confirmed the order).

12) Jan Molyneaux (my agent), wrote to Mr. John Atkinson (Head of Legal & Member Services) 11th. September 1997, regarding the decision made by the Inspector as to the route of the Path. Requesting Mr. Atkinson to confirm that the Council do not agree that the line of the path is covered by my new house. (Appendix 7), having received no reply, another letter was sent 24th. September 1997, requesting a reply by 7th. October 1997. A reply was received 11th. October 1997, too late to take further action.

13) After the BCC. had confirmed that the path existed, MBDC. issued an order to remove the path. The order received objections (Not by BCC), and a public inquiry was called for 9th. February 1999, to be presided over by an Inspector appointed by the Secretary of State. At the inquiry MBDC asked that the order be confirmed and supplied evidence to support their claim. On the very day of the inquiry, an officer (Mr Hall) from BCC attended and objected to the order. BCC had not informed anyone that they would attend. MBDC officers were surprised at the action of the BCC officers after receiving confirmation that BCC would not object. (Appendix 8). It was later discovered that this was because Mr. Clarke of "Bedfordshire Rights of Way Association (BRoWA) had contacted Mr. Hall (BCC). Requesting advice on how to Thwart the order. The Inspector would not confirm the order, (Probably because the BCC. changed their mind and objected to the order at the very last minute) to the surprise and disappointment of MBDC. (The officials changed their minds and objected without consulting Elected Members of the Council) and without informing

me and the MBDC, it is not known if this was sanctioned by the Legal Department within the BCC.

14) I wrote to the Local Government Ombudsman, complaining about the behaviour of BCC. The Ombudsman informed me that BCC had the right to change their mind.

Over the next few months, I requested BCC to arrange a meeting, to discuss the situation. They were reluctant to meet.

15) In January 2000, BCC summoned me to Court for closing the gates at the front of my house. I had obtained permission to erect the gates but BCC informed me that if I closed the gates, they would take me to court because I would be obstructing the footpath even though it was not accessible. At the same time BCC solicitor, contacted my solicitor, stating that I had been abusive to one of the BCC staff. This was later withdrawn and an apology was given stating that the incident did not occur. (Appendix 9)

16) I attended Bedford Magistrates Court 20th. Jan. 2000, in answer to the summons issued by BCC. Before the case began the Barrister for BCC approached me and informed me that if I pleaded not guilty, they would ask for costs, which would amount to a small fortune, and advised me to plead guilty. I represented myself and explained to the Magistrates the situation regarding the Footpath. (Appendix 9a). The Magistrates informed me that unfortunately they had to find me guilty and imposed a fine of £50. The Barrister for BCC then asked for £2366 costs. The Magistrates only awarded £100. This case resolved nothing and it was obvious that the Magistrates were restricted as to what they could do.

17) MBDC advised me to apply to them to have the path extinguished using the Highways Act. An application was presented. MBDC met 6th. September 2000 where the members voted to apply to have the path extinguished using the Highways Act. This was in spite of the BCC saying they would object.

18) BCC Development Control Committee met 14th. September 2000, to discuss Footpath 28. The committee members were asked to create a new path on my land, the committee were also informed that MBDC were to issue on order to extinguish the path. The members voted not to create a new path but to support MBDC in their efforts to remove the path. After the meeting Mr. Brawn BCC approached me saying **"Congratulations Mr. Bowers no hard feelings"** the decision of the committee was confirmed by BCC to me and MBDC. a few days later. (Appendix 10)

19) MBDC issued an order to extinguish the path, which received objections from various user groups. Because of the objections a public Inquiry was arranged 19th. June 2001. The inquiry was presided over by an Inspector appointed by The Secretary of State. MBDC employed the services of a Barrister who stated the case for MBDC for the order to be confirmed, it was also supported by Maulden Parish Council and Bedfordshire Police Authority and various local people. BCC did not attend. At the beginning of the proceedings a letter was produced by Mr. Clarke of the "Bedfordshire Rights of Way Association". The letter, dated 13th. June 2001, was written by Mr.Brawn BCC to Mr. Clarke referring to the meeting held 14th. September 2000, stating that BCC did not support the order. (Appendix 11). This was contrary

to the statement made by Mr. Brawn September 2000(Appendix 8). It is not known if this letter was approved by BCC or Mr. Brawn had taken it upon himself to write to Mr. Clarke stating that the BCC were not supporters of the order. This confirms the collusion between BCC officers and user groups. There is much evidence of collusion and closeness of BCC officers and user groups. In a letter dated 12th. July 2000, Brawn to Mike (BRWA) he states that we, (BCC) are determined to retain Footpath 28! Also, a personal E.mail. dated 10th. August 2007, Mike (BRWA) to Martyne (BCC) discussing me (Appendix 11).

20) It would appear that Mr. Clarke attended the inquiry representing BCC in their effort to persuade the Inspector not to confirm the order. It needs to be confirmed who in BCC authorised this action. It appears that the officers and their allies were absolutely opposed to the creation of a **Precedent!**

The inquiry lasted a whole day, and it appeared from statements given that the Inspector would confirm the order. This was the opinion of most people present.

21) Nothing was heard until 13th. August, when a nearby neighbour phoned me to say they had received a letter from the Inspector to say that he would not be confirming the order. MBDC; and myself, as well as other supporters of the order were not informed of the Inspectors decision until days later. In a letter dated 16th. August, the Inspector apologised for not informing me earlier. (Appendix 12). In his report the Inspector stated that BCC did not support the order. This could only have been because of the letter produced the day of the inquiry.

22) I met with MBDC officers to discuss the situation; they stated that they were surprised and disappointed at the decision of the Inspector. It was the unanimous opinion of all present that the action of BCC needed to be questioned, and advised me to write to the Chief Executive of BCC asking them to explain their actions. I wrote to the Chief Executive 19th. September 2001 saying that the minutes of the meeting held 14th.September 2000 did not reflect the feelings of the members. (As stated in Mr. Brawns letter).

I received a reply 28th. September 2001 in which the Chief Executive after consulting the Council solicitor (Possibly John Atkinson), stated *"At no stage did the Committee "as a body" formally support the proposal of MBDC to extinguish footpath 28 Maulden"*. (Appendix 13). This was in complete contrast to the opinion of Mr. Brawn in his letter dated September 2000 where he stated *"The committee voted in favour of the extinguishment"* (Appendix 8).

NOTE! It was later discovered (through the Freedom of Information Act) that the Chief Executive (Mr. Bell) had written to the Ombudsman, 31st. October 2000 (Appendix 13) stating that the Committee had in fact voted to support the MBDC. In the same letter he stated that *"My Council believes that the Bridleway near to Footpath 28 is a suitable alternative route and, as a result the Footpath is not needed for public use. My officers will therefore, not take any physical action to open the path or recommend further legal action to make the landowner do so"*.

23) The Development Control Committee met 6th. December 2001 and after a long discussion the members agreed that the minutes of the meeting held 14th. September did not

reflect the true wishes of the members. The members also voted to extinguish Footpath 28. At the next meeting, 24th. January 2002, the members instructed the council to issue an order to extinguish the path. This was confirmed by Mr. Brawn in a letter to me stating that an order would be issued within 2 months. (Appendix 14), MBDC council also confirmed the intentions of BCC and that they fully supported the order.

I received a letter from BCC 1st. March 2002 informing me that the "Development Control Committee" would be meeting in private 7th. March 2002 to discuss Footpath 28, (Appendix 15) I was also informed that I could not attend and I could not have a representative to attend.

30) I received a letter dated 11th. March 2002 informing me that the committee had changed their minds and did not wish to go ahead with the extinguishment. (Appendix 16) no reason was given at that time. It was revealed at a meeting 16th. March 2005 by Mr. Brawn and Kevin Ward that at the private meeting held 7th. March 2002 the members of the Committee were threatened by officers of BCC. that they would have legal action taken against them individually, if they continued to extinguish Footpath 28. (This is the reason the members changed their minds.).

31) I received a letter dated 19th. July 2002, from BCC. Informing me that they intend to recommend to the "Development Control Committee" that they create a new path through my property.

The committee met 31st. October 2002, the members voted not to accept the officer's recommendation but to enquire about the possibility of upgrading the nearby Bridleway in an attempt to extinguish Footpath 28.

32) At a meeting 6th.March 2003, the committee suggested various options to upgrade the Bridleway.

   I received a letter from BCC 19th. November 2003, informing me, that BCC intends to request the members attending a meeting 27th. November 2003 to revoke the resolution made at the meeting 6th. March 2003 to upgrade Bridleway 24, and to create a path through my property.   This was because they had received a complaint from the "Open Spaces Society" stating that they would take Legal action against BCC if they pursued the option of upgrading the Bridleway (Appendix 17). The members voted to revoke their previous decision.

33) Prior to a meeting, held 4th. March 2004, the committee members made a site visit to my property, also present were two Parish Councillors who were present at my request.

   While the members were at the property, Mr. Brawn was asked if the members would like to see the alternative route nearby (The Bridleway). Mr. Brawn stated that it was "irrelevant," when asked if the members were aware of a letter from the Police Authority objecting to a new path being created, Mr. Brawn replied it was "irrelevant". (It is evident that Mr. Brawn could help in further enquires).

34) At the meeting, the members were given the choice of 5 options where to create a new path. The officers recommended one going through the centre of my property. This was the route requested by "Open Spaces

Society". The Maulden Parish Council, and MBDC as well as the Police Authority objected to any new path being created. (Appendix 18) The members went against the officer's recommendation and chose the only common-sense option available to them.

35) I contacted my Local MP, Mr. Jonathon Sayeed to make him aware of the actions of BCC, A meeting was arranged to meet with Mr. Sayeed where he was made aware of the situation, he stated that it was "unbelievable", and suggested he made a complaint to the Local Government Ombudsman.

I supplied Mr. Sayeed with all relevant documents, and they were sent to the Ombudsman asking to have the case investigated. After a few weeks the Ombudsman replied stating "They could only investigate anything that had happened in the past twelve months". (Appendix 19)

36) BCC issued an order to create a new path, which was advertised in the Local Paper 23rd. July 2004, stating anyone wishing to object should do so in writing by 30th. August 2004. The order was objected to by MBDC; Maulden Parish Council; and nearly 200 private individuals; BCC. officers wrote to most of the private individuals requesting them to withdraw their objections. (Appendix 20).

37) I met with the Rights of Way Officer for MBDC. (Siobhan Vincent). It was agreed that the way forward was to apply to BCC to have the path extinguished using Highways Act 118, and also to apply using Highways Act 116, (Highways Act 116 is determined in a Magistrates Court). I sent the application to BCC. 11th. September 2004. BCC responded, 12th. October 2004 acknowledging the application, stating

that it would be12-18 months before it could be considered. (Appendix 21).

38) Sunday 10th. October 2004 the "Sunday Telegraph" devoted a quarter of a page publicising my situation stating that the situation was political in so much that BCC had changed their minds twice at the last minute at public inquires. (Appendix 22)

39) I wrote to the Chief Executive BCC, 2nd. November 2004, requesting a meeting with the appropriate people to discuss my applications. I received a reply 15th. November 2004 informing me that the matter was now in the hands of Mr.Tim Malynn who would be in contact with me.

I tried to contact Mr.Malynn by telephone 31st. November 2004, and was informed that Mr.Malynn was not available, I requested to speak to anyone else concerning the matter, and was told that there was nobody available

I asked if I could leave a message for someone to contact me. I later received a call from a Mr. Clive Beckett, who informed me that there was no point in having a meeting to discuss the applications because they would not be considered for at least two years; he also added that BCC are reluctant to take applications to Magistrates Court. I requested that a letter be sent to me to that effect. Mr. Beckett stated that a letter had already been sent to me.

I received the letter 5th. December 2004, postmarked 3rd. December 2004. (Appendix 23). (Letter dated 26th. November)

40) I wrote to the Chief Executive 27th. December 2004 expressing my dissatisfaction and requested that a meeting be arranged.

I received a letter 20th.January 2005, from Mrs. Sally Wileman (Appendix 24) giving the reasons why I had received the letter from Mr. Malynn many days after they said it had been sent. She also informed me that, Mr. Clive Beckett had in fact agreed to meet me (It would seem strange for me to turn down a meeting after I had requested it).

I contacted Mrs. Wileman by phone and found her very pleasant and helpful. Mrs. Wileman told me that she could see no reason why a meeting could not be arranged, and said that she would arrange a meeting at a time suitable for all parties. Mrs. Wileman wrote to me 16th. March 2005, stating that a meeting had been arranged, for 23rd. March 2005.

41) I attended the meeting, accompanied by three councillors who had always supported me in the past.

The meeting was presided over by BCC. officers, Mr. Kevin Ward and Mr. Brawn. The possibility of having the path extinguished was discussed at length, Mr. Brawn revealed that, at the private meeting held 7th. March 2002, members were threatened with legal action if they persisted in trying to remove the path. Mr. Kevin Ward suggested that they should approach MBDC to see if they would consider using the Town & Country Act to remove the path because the development (my house) was not complete. This is what BCC advised in 1997 and then objected to the order. (I was not happy with the situation).

42) I received a letter from Mr.Brawn 23rd. June 2005 stating that they did not wish to act upon the proposals discussed at the meeting of 23rd. March 2005. I received a letter from BCC 10th. August 2005, informing me that they intend to forward the order to the Inspectorate to confirm the order to create a new path. (Appendix 25).

43) I contacted Nadine Dorries MP, the new MP for the area to arrange a meeting to make her aware of his situation. A meeting was arranged for 21st. October 2005. My next-door neighbour accompanied me, after Mss. Dorries MP had been made aware of the situation she said it is "Ludicrous" and that she would look into the matter.

44) I received a letter from the Inspectorate 20th. January 2006 informing him that a Public Inquiry would take place 9th. March 2006, at Ampthill.

The Beds. County Council received many objections to their order after it was advertised in the Local paper. Objections were from Mid. Beds. District Council, Maulden, Parish Council, Police Authority and 200 private objections from members of the public. Beds. County Council Officers contacted approx. 180 members of the public, asking them to reconsider their objection, at the same time writing to the Local Authorities threatening them with legal action if they continued to object. Maulden Parish Council replied stating that they were appalled at the threat and stated they would continue to object. Mid. Beds. District Council however conceded to the threat and withdrew their objection 8th. February 2006. (Appendix 26)

45) The inquiry, on 9th. March 2006 was presided over by an Inspector appointed by the Secretary of State, her name

was Mrs. Erica Eden. (This Inspector was subject to an Inquiry over a similar case she chaired in Dorset, and as a result was ordered not to preside over any further inquiries.)

During the course of the Inquiry, I was halted halfway through my statement by the Inspector. who said, **"I have heard enough"**, although I had spent many hours preparing the statement I was not allowed to continue. The Inquiry was split into two days and concluded on 28th. March 2006. At the very end of the Inquiry, Mr. Brawn, of the Beds. County Council, stated that he disagreed with evidence included in my statement.

46) I wrote to Mr. Brawn 29th. March 2006 asking him to identify, any part of my statement, which he considered incorrect. Mr, Brawn replied 3rd. April 2006 stating that "He did not consider it would be helpful or a good use of his time to get into a detailed discussion concerning the contents of the statement". I wrote to the Chief Executive of Beds. County Council expressing my dissatisfaction at the response I had received from Mr. Brawn. I received a reply from Mr. Kevin Ward (For the Chief Executive) 20th. April, saying that they had no wish to get into any lengthy discussion, and they had no more to add. I again wrote to the Chief Executive requesting a more positive reply. I received a reply from Mr. Tim Maylynn (For the Chief Executive) saying they had no more to add. (Appendix 27)

47) I then wrote to the Local Government Ombudsman complaining about the attitude of Beds. County Council's to my request. The LGO. Suggested I contacted the Planning Inspector. I contacted the Planning Inspector and was told there was nothing they could do. (Appendix 28)

48) I was summoned to Court at Bedford on 9th. August 2007, Beds County Council issued the summons because Footpath 28 was obstructed. (Chief Executive for Beds. County Council Mr.Bell informed the Local Government Ombudsman on 31st. October 2000. *"My Council believe that the Bridleway near to Footpath 28 is a suitable alternative route and, as a result the Footpath is not needed for public use. My officers will therefore, not take any physical action to open the path or recommend further legal action to make the landowner do so".* (Appendix 13)

49) When I attended court, I asked that the case be Dismissed because there were two applications submitted in 2004 to remove the Path, which had not been processed. The solicitor representing Beds. County Council, stated that the council had no intention of processing the applications and that it was a delaying tactic being used by me. (Appendix 29). (Although the Beds. County Council had confirmed to me that it would take up to 18months to 2 years to process the applications).

The Magistrates considered that the case was too complicated for them and that a circuit Judge should consider the case.

50) I received a letter from Mr. Brawn of BCC. Stating that they had no intention of processing my applications to remove the path. (Appendix 29)

51) I attended court 2nd. November 2007 accompanied by 3 Councillors and a past Councillor who attended to support me. The Judge would not let them give evidence, and refused me the opportunity of questioning Council

Officers even though I had spent many hours preparing my case. The Judge also refused to have a SITE visit, which I had requested.

52) I was not fined but had to pay £1000 costs and was issued with an enforcement order to remove any obstacles from the line of the path. (These included large trees and bushes, a stable block and sheds. and fencing.).

53) I had a meeting with my local MP. Nadine Dorries MPshe informed him that the BCC. Would soon be disbanded and that a unitary Council would replace them who could be more sympathetic and understanding.

54) My local Councillor arranged for a meeting to be held at my home, 10th. June 2008, the meeting was to include a director of the BCC. and others to see the situation for themselves. The director, Charlie McNally stated that LOGIC needed to be applied to the situation.

55) A meeting was arranged to discuss the situation on 21st August 2008 at County Hall Bedford. I was accompanied by three councillors, who wished to support me. During the course of the meeting it was suggested by the officer's present that I should apply to BCC. To have the path "DELETED" using Section 53 of The Wildlife and Countryside Act. It was also revealed that Committee Members were threatened by officers at the Private Meeting which took place 7th. March 2002, that, legal actions would be taken against them if they continued to try and remove the path.

Councillors present stated, that they were disgusted that members should have been (Blackmailed).

When the minutes of the meeting were issued, I contested the contents of the minutes and requested to see a copy of the written minutes taken by a lady present at the meeting. I was informed that *"Unfortunately the original minutes had been destroyed"*. The Director present at the meeting left the BCC a few weeks later. (Appendix 30).

56) My local Councillor, Alan Carter, requested BCC, that my application issued in 2004 be bought before the Committee to be considered, but was informed that they had no intention of doing so. However, the committee met on 5th. March 2009, without informing me and in the absence of Councillor Carter (Who had previously given his apologies for absence) also without being informed of recent significant changes made, and it was decided not to process my applications. The BCC was disbanded later in the month.

57) I appeared before the same Judge (Nicholas Leigh-Smith) on 20th. April 2009 because the obstacles had not been removed from the path. A barrister represented me; the case was heard over two days. When questioned by my barrister, Mr. Brawn of BCC, stated that the *"Obvious common-sense thing to do was to Extinguish the path"* when asked why that had not been done! Mr. Brawn replied, *"We have gone past the common-sense stage"*. When question by the Judge, to explain, Mr. Brawn said, *"If the council were to look at the situation AFRESH, they would recommend that the path be Extinguished"*.

After taking the oath, Councillor Alan Carter remarked, *"I am ashamed to be associated with BCC. because of the way the Officers of the council and User Groups had colluded with each other against Mr. Bowers"*. The barrister representing the BCC said to Councillor Carter, *"I am going to give you the opportunity to retract that remark"*, Councillor Carter held up the oath card and replied, *"I have just sworn to tell the truth and that is what I am doing"*. The Judge remarked, *"That is hearsay"*.

58) After two days of debate and questioning the Judge announced that he would give his decision on 30th. April 2009.

The Judge found me guilty of the offence of (Unlawfully obstructing a Right of Way) and sentenced me to a fine of £5000 with costs of £9000 and a fine of £250 per. day if the obstructions were not removed. He also informed me that I had not been encouraged by Council Officials to attempt to remove the path. (There is much evidence to prove the opposite). That whole court hearing cost me £19,000. I was advised to appeal but could not afford it.

I was forced to comply with the Judges request.

59) Over the next few months, I had to remove bushes and trees, one of which was 30feet high, also demolish a 200-year-old building, sheds, and re-position a whole stable block together with fencing and other obstacles. I also had to erect 180 metres of fencing to protect my animals and to keep my property private. The total cost was in excess of £10,000. The path was opened up in August 2009.

60) I felt that I had been defeated, until I was made aware of many other homeowners who had suffered a similar fate because of Local Authorities and User Groups. After investigating the situation, it was discovered that the evil

and distress caused by Rights of Way Activists was prevalent throughout the land.

61) I contacted many people who had suffered the same distress and financial burden I had experienced for twenty years. With the information gained through other people, I decided to attempt to get the Imposed Right of Way removed from my property. The new Local Authority in place is Central Bedfordshire Council, who had taken over from Beds. County Council. Many of the Councillors within the new authority had been Councillors for Mid. Beds. District Council, who had always supported me in the past, together, with Maulden Parish Council.

62) In August 2011 the Council installed a gate at one end of the Footpath to stop any children running onto the main road. The gate was installed at the wrong end of the path 180 metres away. When I enquired why they had placed the gate the wrong end of the path, they replied, **"Because the ground was too hard at the correct end"** This was later to be found untrue, (See E.Mail. Dated 14th. November 2012 Gemma Harrison to Mr. Maciejewski.) (Appendix 31)

63) I tried to make contact with Rights of Way Officers of the new Council but found they were reluctant to resurrect the problem associated with Footpath 28. After much persistence I eventually persuaded the Rights of Way officers to meet me and discuss the situation. I also made requests for documents associated with Footpath 28 using the Freedom of Information Act. After seeking advice from Information Commissioners Office and much persistence I eventually gained access to many revealing documents, which indicated the collusion and closeness

of officials with User Groups in their endeavours to create and maintain Rights of Way at any cost.

64) A meeting was arranged with Mr. Maciejewski, Rights of Way officer for Central Beds. on 14th December 2011. I was accompanied by, Mr. Howard Lockey a former Councillor who had always supported me. At the meeting Mr. Maciejewski assured me that he would look into the possibility of processing the applications submitted by me in 2004 and 2008, and assured me that the applications would be treated in an impartial manner and with a fresh approach, and the necessary documents should be in place earlier in the new year. Mr. Maciejewski and other officers interviewed 18 local people who had filled in forms stating that the footpath has never been considered public.

65) Mr. Maciejewski informed me in June 2012 that he was in the process of Drafting the relevant documents to be put before the Council Committee with respect to my applications and it would be at least August before they would be available. The Draft, documents were received by 22nd. August, after examining the documents I made certain comments and returned them to be amended.

66) I made a request for a copy of the agenda and minutes of a meeting held in 1995. A copy of the Agenda was sent to me but I was told there was no copy of the minutes available. I asked for a letter to inform me that the minutes had been lost or destroyed. After a few days I received a copy of the minutes. (Which they did not have). The same thing happened in April 2010 when certain documents were requested. (Appendix 32) (Appendix 3)

67) A meeting was arranged 26th. October 2012, to discuss the contents of the report to be submitted to the committee. The meeting was attended by, Mr. Maciejewski and Central Beds. solicitor Andrew Emerton. I was accompanied by, Councillor Paul Duckett. After much discussion it was agreed that the report to be put before the committee was misleading in many respects.

Further evidence in the form of a letter, written in 1957, by the then Local Authority (Appendix 1). Also, a letter written by Mr. Bell (BCC. CEO) to the Local Government Ombudsman explaining his council's view of the situation (Appendix 13); was presented to Mr. Maciecjewski, who stated that **"It is of little value".** However, Mr. Emerton (Solicitor) whose actions and comments indicated that he was very surprised at the evidence, and enquired where the information was obtained... (Note! Since that information was made available to Mr. Emerton, his general attitude to the situation seems to have changed.)

It was agreed that another meeting should take place to finalise the report. A further meeting was arranged for 8th. November 2012. The meeting was attended by, Mrs. Sally Wileman to take notes, it was also agreed that the report needed further amendments before it was submitted to the committee for consideration.

Mr. Maciejewski amended the report and stated that this was the version to be put before the committee at the meeting to be held 13th. February 2013. I reviewed the report to be presented to the committee and supplied Mr. Maciejwski with certain amendments which I believed should be made before it was presented to the committee.

These amendments were made available to Mr. Maciejwski 15th. January 2013, (Appendix 33); <u>no action was taken</u>! The Local MP Nadine Dorries MP wrote to every member of the committee supporting me. (Appendix 33)

68) At the meeting held 13th.February 2013, Mr. Maciejewski the author of the report presented to the committee recommended that they refuse to approve any of the three applications submitted by myself. The Three applications were:

1/ To delete the path using Section 53 of the Wildlife and Countryside Act 1981, because the path was created in error.

2/ To extinguish the path using Section 118 of the Highways Act, because it was unnecessary for public use.

3/ To stop up the path Using Section 116 of the Highways Act, because there is a suitable alternative route nearby.

The reason Mr. Maciejwski gave for refusing the first application was that there was not sufficient new evidence to support it. (The committee were not made aware of all the evidence provided) the Solicitor present did not inform the members of the difference between the applications. Therefore, the members were not aware of the evidence submitted and the implications, which could arise. Because they were misinformed the members voted not to approve the first application.

The reason Mr. Maciejwski gave for refusing the second application was that the nearby Bridleway was not a suitable alternative route. The former Chief Executive of Beds County Council (in October 2000) had already confirmed that his officers believed that the Bridleway was a suitable alternative route and that the Footpath was not needed for public use. When questioned by members of the committee 13th. February 2013, although reluctant to give an answer (He was asked seven times) Mr. Maciejwski agreed that the Bridleway was a suitable alternative route. Bridleway 24 has also been confirmed as being suitable for public use by The Open Spaces Society in a letter dated, 15th. April 2003. The letter written by Kate Ashbrook, states **"The bridleway is perfectly suitable for public use."**
(Appendix 17)

The reason Mr. Maciejwski gave for refusing the third application was that all the criteria had not been met to apply to the Magistrates Court under Section 116. He also stated that the nearby Bridleway was not a suitable alternative route When asked by members of the committee "How did the public gain access to the same point that the Footpath led to, before the footpath was made available in 2009" after being asked many times, Mr. Maciejwski reluctantly replied that the public had used the Bridleway. He was also asked if there had been any incidents regarding the public using the Bridleway. Mr. Maciejwski informed the committee that he was not aware of any incidents occurring.

69) The members voted against the wishes of the officers and approved the 2nd and 3rd. Applications.

It was also apparent that the members were aware of the history of the 20 years of debate about the Footpath and wished to bring it to a satisfactory conclusion.

After the meeting Mr. Maciejwski and the solicitor Mr. Emerton approached me and congratulated me, and informed me that the appropriate Orders would be issued within two months.

70) Mr. Maciejwski wrote to me 19th.February(Dated March) 2013 expressing his recollections of the committee's resolutions at the meeting held 13th. February 2013. His views were completely alien to the feelings and decisions made by the Committee Members. (Appendix 34)

On reading the letter; I, Mr.Connaughton, and former Councillor Lockey who were all present at the meeting, informed the Chairman of the Committee that the views expressed in Mr. Maceijwski's letter were not true, and that the minutes of the meeting should record the true proceedings of the meeting.(Appendix 34a)(5)..

71) I received a Decision letter from Mr. Maceijwski 9th.April 2013 outlining the printed minutes of the meeting held 13th. February 2013. (Appendix 35).

The minutes stated that the Committee resolved NOT to approve the application submitted by me, to DELETE the path. This was because the officers informed them that I had not supplied sufficient evidence to support my application.

The officers and solicitor were aware of important evidence and documents, which had been submitted, but had failed to make them available to the members and also failed to direct the members on the legal aspects of the application. (The members were therefore Misinformed by the officers and attending solicitor)

A second application submitted by me to EXTINGUISH the path was approved by the committee.

However, the minutes also stated that the members of the committee agreed that I should pay for any additional work to be carried out on the nearby Bridleway.

NOTE! There was no proposal made, and no vote taken with regard to payment of any work to be carried out.

A third application submitted by me to STOP up the path (Using Magistrates Court) was approved by the Committee. However, the minutes stated that the Members of the committee agreed that I should pay for any additional work to be carried out on the nearby Bridleway. NOTE! There was no proposal made and no vote taken with regard to payment of any work to be carried out.

Myself, and others made the Chief Executive and officers aware of their concern regarding the accuracy of the contents of the minutes.

72) I contacted a Mrs. Bell who had taken the minutes during the meeting, asking for a copy of the original minutes taken. I was informed that the handwritten minutes taken at the meeting had been destroyed. (Appendix 36).

Because it was considered that the members of the committee held 13th. February 2013, were not made aware of the full facts regarding the first application to

DELETE the path. It was requested by me, and others that the committee should meet to reconsider the decision NOT to approve the application, also to investigate contents of the minutes as presented to the members. (The minutes presented were exactly as Mr. Maciejewski had predicted 19th. February 2013.)

73) Mr. Maciejewski wrote to me 9th. April 2013, outlining the contents of the minutes of the meeting held 13th. February 2013. These however were an incorrect record of the decisions made by the members.

The minutes do record that the members voted to approve two applications, but it also states that the members wished me to be responsible for any costs incurred for carrying out any work on the nearby Bridleway. (This is completely untrue; the vote was to approve of the applications with no mention of costs).

Mr. Maciejewski also informed me that I would be liable for any legal and administrative costs. Also, if a Barrister was to be employed, I would also have to pay any additional costs.

This was later denied by the Solicitor Mr. Emerton in a letter to me, dated 13th. May 2013. (Appendix 37).

74) Because the application made under the Wildlife and Countryside Act 1981 to delete the path was not approved, I was obliged to submit an Appeal to the Planning Inspectorate within 28 days.

I sent an appeal to the Planning Inspectorate on 30th. April 2013, and informed Central Beds. Council of my intentions. (Appendix 38)

75) I made a request to Central Beds. Council, for certain documents on 27th. March 2013. I was sent some on 25th. April 2013 and informed that one document when "Redacted" would be of little use. I contacted the officer concerned and stated that I would still like to see the document, and I was informed that they were not prepared to send it. After obtaining advice from "The Information Commissioners Office" I asked for an internal review to be carried out by the council for the reason why they would not make the document available. After a few days the "Redacted" document was made available to me.

76) A neighbour of mine showed me a letter he had recently received from Mr. Maciejewski, informing him about work Mr.Maciecjewski proposed to carry out to the nearby Bridleway. The work proposed was completely unnecessary and a waste of money. (Appendix 39)

77) CBC. Issued an order, to EXTINGUISH the path dated 17thMay 2013. It was advertised in the Local Paper, and was also posted both ends of the path. (Appendix 40)

A letter headed "Abuse of Public Office" dated 28th. May 2013 was written to Mr. John Atkinson (Head of Legal and Democratic Services) expressing concern about the present situation regarding the removal of Footpath 28. (Appendix 41)

I wrote to the Chief Executive of the Council 3rd. June 2013 requesting him to investigate the actions of officers within his Authority. (Appendix 42)

78) CBC. Issued an order, to STOP UP the path dated 13th. June 2013. It was advertised in the Local Paper, and posted both ends of the path. The order was to be considered at Bedford Magistrates Court 17th. July 2013. (Appendix 43).

79) Having had no response from the Chief Executive, I wrote again 21st. June 2013, expressing my concern regarding the actions of officer's under his control. (Appendix 44)
See also Attached Confidential Letter and Letter from DC. Broadhurst Dorset CID.
I also contacted John Atkinson (Legal Advisor) requesting a meeting to discuss the situation.

80) I attempted to speak to The Chief Executive's office 2nd. July 2013 at 9.56am. After a very long wait I was put through to John Atkinson, during a brief discussion, Mr. Atkinson informed me that the Chief Executive would be contacting me in the next few days, he also stated "We are not prepared to meet with you" I enquired "Who are we?" Mr. Atkinson replied "The Chief Executive".

81) The Chief Executive responded 3rd. July 2013 to my letter of 3rd. June 2013 in which he states **"The Development Management Committee found insufficient evidence"**.

Note! They were informed by the officers that there was insufficient evidence. Fact! The officers and legal advisors were in possession of much new evidence but it was withheld from the committee members. The CEO also states that **"As a matter of law, there is no facility for the decision of the Development Management Committee to be reviewed in any other way"**. It will be seen that the CEO has been asked to reveal what law he refers to many times; but has been unable or unwilling to provide it. (Appendix 45).

82) I responded to the CEO on 4th. July 2013 informing him that the minutes of the meeting of DMC 13th. February 2013 were incorrect. I also informed him that the reconvening of committee's had taken place in the past and enclosed evidence. Because of statements made in his letter, I enclosed certain documents showing that Misconduct/ Malfeasance was and is taking place in his Authority. (Appendix 46).

83) I attended the Court Hearing with respect to the Section 116 order, on 17th. July 2014 I was accompanied by Councillor Paul Ducket (Ward Councillor). The Council Solicitor Mr. Sutton, requested the Court to adjourn the hearing. Although I had requested many times to meet with the Council to discuss the case, they had always refused to meet with me. The Court granted an adjournment until 15th. January 2015 (Appendix 47) Councillor Duckett suggested to Mr.Sutton that we should all meet to discuss the situation. (Although requested many times after, the council refused to meet)

84) Reviewing documents relating to Schedule 14 Appeal to Secretary of State. An inappropriate document was discovered. It was an E.mail dated 8th. August 2013, sent by Mr. Maciejewski of Central Beds. Council, to Mrs. Jean McEntee of the Inspectorates Office. It was addressed "Dear Jean" and Signed "Kind regards Adam" which indicates a closeness between the two parties. It also contained derogatory remarks about me. (Appendix 48)

85) I received a response to my letter of 4th. July 2013, from Mr. Emerton (Solicitor) on behalf of CEO. dated 22nd. August 2013. (Appendix 49). He states: **No objections were made to minutes of DMC meeting.** ...I and others who attended the meeting contested the minutes before the Committee approved them. See various letters (Appendix 34a). He also makes reference to Information I made available to CEO referring to "Misconduct in Public Office" in the form of booklets, but has not made any comments about information contained in the Booklets. He also states that the CEO has stated that the decision of the Committee cannot be revisited, but again refuses to give any lawful reason why.

He also states Para. 3 line 6 **"The request to reconsider the decision has not affected, or been affected by, the appeal".** Note! In previous correspondence it is stated that the Committee cannot reconsider its decision because an appeal has been made. (Appendix 50).

86) Through the efforts of Councillor Duckett and myself we eventually had a meeting with the Councils "Customer Relations Team" 12th. September 2013, where we provided the team with much evidence and made an official complaint about the actions and conduct of various officers and officials.

87) Mr. Connaughton received a letter from John Atkinson, in response to a letter sent 5th. & 17th. October 2013, in which Mr. Connaughton requested answers to several questions. Mr. Atkinson states **"I appreciate that the history of this matter is important in providing evidence regarding the existence of a public right way or otherwise. However, at this juncture, I am not prepared to engage in correspondence with you about**

the historical evidence or the rights and wrongs of this matter" (Appendix 50.1)

88) I received a reply 25th. October 2013 regarding complaint made to Customer Relations Team (Appendix 51), as was expected it was a case of officers investigating their colleagues'. I sent a response by E.mail. (Appendix 51a). In response to my E.mail they confirmed that the officers do not wish to discuss the situation.

89) After advice from ICO and many requests to examine the file on Footpath 28, eventually the council agreed to allow me access to the file. I attended the Council offices in Shefford on 18th. December 2013. I was shown into a room where the files were placed upon a table. As soon as I saw the files it was obvious, they were not the Council files. All the file holders were new, and all the documents had been copied the day before 17th. December 2013. I stated that they were not the files I expected, but was informed they were the only ones available. I spent seven hours examining the files and discovered that they had been pre-selected and many were missing. I informed the officer who was present in the room (David Leverington, Rights of Way Officer) that it was obvious some documents were missing. He again said **"they are the only documents available.".** Mr. Leverington left the room for a while. I later discovered he had contacted Adam Maciejewski to inform him that I believed some documents were missing. When I returned home in the evening I had received an E.mail from Mr. Maciejewski 10.42am. in which he states, *"Further to your conversation with Mr. Leverington I believe that the following E.mail you requested to see in its entirety. You will see I have removed the two pages as they only contained the antivirus disclaimers. I have done this to a*

number of other E.mails in the folder to save you having to (Appendix 52)

This indicates that AM must have spent a considerable amount of time (Hours) 17/12/13, examining the file, and removing certain documents before printing them to present to me for examination.

I spent the next two days analysing the documents I had copied at the council offices. The documents revealed the actions and feelings of some of the Council Officers. I was particularly surprised at the comments and actions of two particular officers. Namely: Sally Wileman and Ernest Sutton (Solicitor), these two officers had always appeared very pleasant and impartial. However, on reading information contained in the documents, I realise they are not as I believed.

90) Mr. Sutton phoned me 30th. December 2013 asking my advice on how to approach the Magistrates Court hearing to be heard 15th. January 2015. I suggested we meet to discuss the situation. Because I had not heard from CBC, I contacted them and was advised that the case would be deferred and that they would inform me Tuesday 14th. January 2014. Mr Sutton also advised me that it would not be necessary to attend court because they were requesting another adjournment. The court granted the Council another adjournment until September 2014. Because I had not received any communication from the Council, I contacted Mr. Sutton 22nd January 2014 who assured me he would contact Melanie Clay (Monitoring Officer) and arrange a meeting to discuss the situation. I eventually received a copy of the Notice of new hearing.11th. February 2014 (Appendix 53).

91) 2nd. February 2014, I wrote to CEO insisting that we meet to discuss the situation, I also informed him that the council had not been in contact with me concerning the adjournment requested by Mr. Sutton at the court hearing 15th. January 2014. (Appendix 54). Response received 7th. February 2014 (Appendix 54a).

92) Because the Council refused to answer questions put to them. Mr. Connaughton wrote a very informative letter to CEO. 12th. February2014 insisting that they respond and answered the questions previously asked. (Appendix 55).

93) On 14th. February 2014 I again wrote to the CBC (Delivered by hand) requesting information regarding my request for a report from the Customer Relation Team; also requesting details of the statement of case they propose to present regarding the Section 116 order they have presented to the Magistrates Court. I addressed this letter to the Access for Information Department because the officials refuse to meet with me. (Appendix 56).

94) I received a response to my request 3rd. March 2014. Stating that they will not disclose the information I requested. They also stated that they will not respond to any further requests I make to them, because they consider I am being VEXATIOUS. (Appendix 57)

95) Mr. Connaughton wrote again to CEO 4th. March 2014 (Appendix 58) in response to a letter received from CEO dated 28th.February 2014. (Appendix 58a) again, requesting answers to questions previously asked. Mr. Connaughton also wrote a very informative letter again to the CEO 7th. March 2014 (Appendix 59) requesting answers.

96) 10th. March 2014 I wrote to Melanie Clay Chief Legal Officer again requesting a meeting to discuss my situation also informing her that the report submitted by her predecessor John Atkinson was out of date and incorrect. (Appendix 60). I received a negative response. 21st. March 2014; but, was informed that Mr. Sutton will arrange a meeting. (Appendix 60a).

22nd. March 2014, I wrote again to Ms. Clay expressing my disappointment that the council still refuse to meet with me. I also asked other questions regarding remarks made by CEO and other officers, reminding her that she was the lawyer and should be able to inform me of reasons why the council are reluctant to meet or answer questions. (Appendix 61).

97) Having had no response to my letter; on 17th. April 2014, I phoned the office of Ms. Clay and spoke to a lady called Lynn Wade (PA). I enquired why I had not received a response to my letter dated 22nd. March 2014. Ms. Wade assured me she would make enquires and phone me back. Having received no communications, I phoned again on 22nd. April 2014, Ms. Wade assured me that a letter of acknowledgement had been sent 17th. March 2014. (I never received this letter). I received a letter from Ms.Clay dated 25th. April 2014; received 28th. April 2014. (By E.Mail)(Appendix 62)(62a) the written copy was not received until 30th. April 2014.

Note! I believe the letter was written by Ms.Wileman and it was signed by Ms.Clay.

They still refuse to answer basic questions put to them.

Note! The council seem rather confused! In an E.mail from Sally Wileman, dated 29th. April. (Appendix 63) she refers to a letter from Ms. Clay dated 28th. April. It can be assumed that the letter dated 25th. April was written 28th. April. (Still refuse to answer questions) and state WE have nothing further to add to that response.

98) I attended a meeting with Mr. Sutton and Sally Wileman. 11th.April 2014. I was accompanied by Councillor Paul Duckett and I insisted that the meeting be recorded. Ms. Wileman insisted that we only discussed the forthcoming Public Inquiry relating to Section 118 order due to be heard 11th. June 2014. I stated that I had not been made aware of any case the council proposed to present at the Inquiry and, who would be presenting the case.

Mr. Sutton informed me that they were employing a Barrister and an expert witness but did not indicate who they were. At the meeting I asked both Mr. Sutton and Ms. Wileman certain questions regarding information I had discovered when I examined the files 18th. December 2014. Both appeared uneasy and could not or would not answer my questions.

99) I was informed in a "Bundle" from Adam Maciejewski that the Barrister to be employed by the Council to present their case at the Section 118 Public Inquiry 11th. June would be Cain Ormanroyd and the expert witness would be Dr. Steven Hollowell. I made enquiries about them both and found: Cain Ormanroyd was a member of "Open Spaces Society" and represented them in retaining "Rights of Way". Note! Open spaces Society is one of the objectors to the Section 118 order. Dr. Steven Hollowell is a former Rights of Way officer from

Cambridgeshire and lectures the "The Ramblers" on how to discover and retain Rights of Way.

Therefore, neither of them can be considered independent or impartial. Because the council will not meet with me, I can only attend the Inquiry and see what sort of case they present.

100) Mr. Connaughton wrote to both Ms. Clay 29th.May 2014 and also to Mr. J. Jamieson (Leader of the Council) 25th. May 2014 expressing his views and again requesting answers to his previous questions. (Appendix 64) and (65).

101) The Chairman of the Committee (Councillor Matthews) and two Ward Councillors met with me 4th. June 2014. We discussed the situation and they agreed to try and reconvene the Committee to reconsider its decision regarding Section 53 to delete the path. Councillor Matthews contacted me 10th. June 2014 and advised me that he had attempted to meet with Ms.Clay but she was not available. In her absence he contacted a Mr. Paul Jones and informed him of his intentions and suggested that an independent officer should produce a report to be placed before the committee.

102) The Local Newspaper "Bedford on Sunday" had shown an interest in the situation and contacted Nadine Dorries MP, who issued a very strongly worded statement in support of my case. Copy of statement next page:

"I became involved with Alan's case and Footpath 28 even before I was an MP and very shortly after I had been selected as a candidate for Mid-Bedfordshire, in April 2005. Alan was in fact the very first constituent I visited at home.

"Quite simply, Footpath 28 should not be there"

"I have written seemingly countless representations on Alan's behalf to local and central government, we have held meetings in my surgeries, at Alan's home, planning inquires and on one memorable occasion in the cafe` of Bedford Hospital.

"At times I have actually been more worried about Alan's health than the footpath, such was the degree of stress I could see he was under. I was so worried that he may have a nervous breakdown or, even worse, a heart attack that on one occasion we almost had a row as I tried to persuade him to abandon his campaign for the sake of his health and that of his wife. I felt it would be better to be alive with the footpath than die in the battle. Alan and I would never fall out, but on that occasion we strongly disagreed and, surprisingly, he won.

"The behaviour of the former County Council claiming the route of Footpath 28 was abhorrent and totally against common sense, given that there is a perfectly serviceable bridleway just a short distance away leading to exactly the same point.

"The disturbing way that staff of the former County Council went about dealing with Alan and forcing the path onto the definitive map was one of several reasons that led me to campaign for the subsequent switch to the current unitary authority and Central Bedfordshire Council. One of the best performing councils in the country.

"The former county council was remote, badly managed, officious and unaccountable and the imposition of footpath 28 is symbolic of the way the staff of former CC behaved.

"It appears that the route of Footpath 28 was claimed as part of a wider ideological campaign to open up as much of the countryside as possible to the general public. To a limited extent I support this, but in Alan's case it led to a ludicrous loss of perspective on behalf of county council staff, given the adjacent, perfectly safe and serviceable path that can be used by anyone who wants to.

"I feel very strongly that no member of the public should have to bear the immense cost of righting the wrongs imposed on them by the incompetence and vindictiveness of local council officials.

"Of the various options for the closure of Alan's case at this point, I would not support extinguishing the path as this denies the liability that exists on the part of the old County Council for its wrongful imposition. The path should be deleted and then a court can decide once and for all where the blame lies and, crucially, how and to what extent Alan should be compensated.

"I only hope that this happens quickly and efficiently with the least amount of stress possible. I still worry about Alan's health and when we can finally say this is all over, I will be the first person stood on his doorstep with a bottle of champagne to celebrate. In the last nine and a half years, one or another of my staff members and I have always been monitoring and managing this case and we will all be happy to toast Alan's victory.

Nadine Dorries MP   28th. May 2014

103) I attended the Public Inquiry regarding Section 118 Highways Act. 11th. June 2014. I made myself known to the Barrister (Cain Ormanroyd) and the expert witness Dr. Hollowell. Although the council had employed them both to present the case to the Inspector, this was the first time I had met with them and had not been communicated by them. Because the council had refused to meet with me, to discuss the case, this was the first opportunity I had to communicate with them. I informed the Barrister that I wished to make an opening statement to the Inspector. At the start of the Inquiry I presented my statement (Appendix 67). I informed the Inspector that I wished to make the statement under oath; he replied **"it is not necessary"**. However, I produced a bible and gave my statement under oath. (My reason for this was because I did not consider the Inquiry was a Fair and Impartial Tribunal; as I have witnessed before).

104) The Inquiry lasted the whole day, and most people present believed the Inspector would confirm the order.

On 27th. June 2014, I again wrote to Ms. Clay, (Delivered by hand) requesting a positive reply to previous letters and again requesting answers to various questions. (Appendix 68).

I received a report from Martin Elliot the Inspector who presided at the Public Inquiry. dated 1st. July 2014, stating that he did not confirm the order. (Appendix 69) This appeared to be a very unusual quick decision, but one which I expected. Over the years it has been mine and many others opinion that Inspectors are reluctant to remove Rights of Way, because it would create a precedent, and would be against their ideological belief as former Rights of Way officers.

105) I sent an E.mail to Melanie Clay 16th. July 2014 (Appendix 70) requesting a response to my letter dated 27th. June 2014 also requesting a meeting to discuss the Section 116 court hearing to be held 8th,9th,10th. September 2014.

I received an E.mail from Mr. Sutton 16th.July 2014 (Appendix 71) asking if I wish to have the hearing to be held 8th,9th,10, September 2014 adjourned (this was probably prompted because of the E.mail sent earlier that day to Melanie Clay. (Appendix 70). I replied that I wish the hearing to go ahead and to be involved in preparing a statement of case. (Appendix 71).

29th. July 2014, I telephoned Melanie Clay's office and spoke to Alexis Crossland (New PA) enquiring why I had not received a response to my letter dated 27th. June 2014 and the E.mail sent 16th. July 2014. She appeared very pleasant and helpful but informed me they were not aware of both documents. The letter dated 27th. June 2014 was delivered by hand and the E.mail had been received. I therefore attended her office and produced copies of the documents referred to, also a letter to her, (Appendix 72). She informed me that they had found the E.mail in question and that Sally Wileman was the person that dealt with such matters. I informed Ms.Crossland that I did not trust Ms. Wileman and asked if she would investigate the situation for me. Which she agreed!

I received a telephone call from Mr.Sutton stating that he would arrange a meeting during the week commencing 4th. August 2014 where we hope to discuss the forthcoming hearing, at the Magistrates Court. I had a further telephone call from Mr. Sutton late evening of 7th. August 2014 saying, he would contact me 11th. August 2014; regarding our proposed meeting.

106) Because I had not received any communication from CBC; I telephoned the offices of Alexis Crossland, Melanie Clay, and Sally Wileman on the morning of 8th. August 2014. No one was available, so I left messages for all of them to contact me. I did not receive a reply!

I telephoned Mr. Sutton 10.0am 11th.August 2014 to remind him of our proposed meeting. He replied that he had forgotten but would contact Melanie Clay and contact me.

I received an E.mail from Sally Wileman the same day 11th. August 2014 (Appendix 73) responding to the telephone messages I left on her colleague's phone. She also states she would E.mail me the next day with information regarding the Magistrates Hearing.

107) Because of negative response from CBC, I E.mailed Mr.Sutton 13th. August 2014 (Appendix 74) informing him that I had prepared a list of witnesses I intended to appear at the Court hearing. I also informed him that I will make no further requests to meet with him (My requests have been ignored).

I received an E.mail from Sally Wileman the same day 15.54 13th. August 2014. (Appendix 75). in which she informs me that she is preparing a letter setting out their position regarding the Magistrates Court hearing.

Saying I should receive an E.mail by Friday 15th. August.

I received an E.mail from Ms.Wileman 15th. August 2015 in the form of a letter. (Appendix 76) informing me that the Council intend to request another adjournment of the Court Hearing (This is the third). It appears as if Ms. Wileman is in control of the council officials. Note! Bedford on Sunday newspaper reported the fact that the council intend to request a further adjournment. It appears they were informed before me. It is obvious the Council are reluctant to appear before a Magistrates Court where the officers would be under oath. Mr. Connaughton and I prepared documents for the Magistrates Court expressing my concern over the Councils request; I delivered the documents by hand to Luton Magistrates Court. (Appendix 77). Mr. Connaughton also wrote to the court expressing his views. (Appendix 78)

108) I received a phone call and an E.mail 21st. August 2014 from the Court informing me that the Council had now made a request to the Court for a third. Adjournment. (Appendix 79)

I received an E.mail from the court 26th. August 2014 referring to a previous telephone conversation where I was informed that the Court had refused the council' request for a further adjournment and had vacated the three-day hearing, but had scheduled a Case Management hearing on the 8th. September 2014. (Appendix 80). I phoned Mrs. Datta Ryan at Luton Magistrates Court early Monday 1st. September 2014 and she informed me that the Case Hearing would still be heard 8th. September 2014. However later that day she sent an E.mail 16.42 (Appendix 81) stating the Council had withdrawn the Section 116 application that day.

It was now obvious that the Council had no intention of attending the hearing scheduled for 8,9,10, September 2014. This can be confirmed by evidence contained in the following documents: E.mail dated 25th. February 2013 Maciejewski and E. Sutton. Where he states *"S 116. This is an untried approach and has a stricter test of needing to be "Unnecessary". However, Justices do look at things with "common sense" rather than legislative perspective and are much more likely to be sympathetic to Mr.Bowers situation (IRESPECTIVE OF ANY MASONIC CONNECTIONS). Their layman's approach does lead them to be less predictable than Inspectors. They may be swayed by opposition- possibly more so from local residents than from national groups. Chance of success= 75%" (Appendix 82)* ... Also E.mail from E.Sutton to A.M dated 17th. December 2012. Where Mr. Sutton states. *"Looks like professional* suicide *to me if we appear to capitulate the Bowers camp will be sharpening their knives before we can escape from the venue". (Appendix 83).*

E.mail from Sally Wileman 28th. August 2014 where she states *"I can confirm that we have not prepared a case/submission for the hearing we anticipated to be on 8-10 September. I wrote to you on 15 August and explained our position had changed and we did not intend to go ahead with that hearing"* (Appendix 84). In the E.mail she refers to letter dated15th. August 2014 (Appendix 85). This confirms the Council had no intention of attending a Magistrates Court where the officers and officials of the council would be under oath, which does not apply at Public Inquiry. The council have had 16 months to prepare a statement of case to present to the court. This can be confirmed by information in an E.mail dated 25th. February 2013. AM to ES. Where AM indicates that he and Chris Heard will begin to plan their submission to the Magistrates Court. (Appendix 86).

It appears that the Council in an act of desperation withdrew the Section 116 application at the last moment, because they were refused a third adjournment. They withdrew the application without the authority of the Elected Members of the Develop Management Committee who instructed them to issue the Section 116 order on 13th. February 2013.

Despite many requests to the officers of the council, by myself and others to meet to discuss the case to be submitted to the court, they always refused. They have also refused to answer many questions put to them.

109) 4th September 2014, the Maulden Parish Council wrote a strongly worded letter to the CEO and chairman of the Council expressing their disgust at the actions of the Council. Copy of letter next page:

MAULDEN PARISH COUNCIL

Clerk: Mrs. Lynda Galler
tel & fax: 01525 404617
e-mail: MauldenPC@duckendfarmhouse.plus.com

Duck End Farmhouse
Flitwick Road
Maulden
Bedford
MK45 2BJ

Mr Richard Carr,
Chief Executive Officer,
Central Bedfordshire Council,
Priory House, Monks Walk,
Chicksands, Shefford,
Beds, SG17 5TQ

4th September, 2014

Dear Mr Carr,

Re: Footpath 28 Maulden, Beds.

I have been requested to write and inform you that Maulden Parish Council is opposed to and disgusted by your Council's withdrawal of the application for a Court hearing regarding Footpath 28 which was to commence on 8th September, especially when consideration is given to the amount of time this has taken since the application was made back in June 2013.

My Council feels that the Hearing application has not been dealt with in a fair or reasonable manner or within a reasonable time frame. Your Council has asked for the Hearing to be adjourned twice and understandably on the third occasion the Court refused a further adjournment.

A great deal of organization and work has been involved in preparing for hearing the objective of which was to clarify and obtain a ruling to finally settle this long outstanding matter. An objective on which all parties were agreed.

Your Council's counter-productive decision to now withdraw the application without giving any reason is unacceptable.

My Council formally requests that you urgently look into this matter in order to let it have a full explanation of your Council's actions and the reasons for your Council's withdrawal.

I await your response as soon as possible.

Yours sincerely,

Clerk
cc Cllr Caroline Maudlin Chairman of CBC
cc Mr. A. Bowers

I received an E.mail from Nadine Dorries MP offering her full support for my case, also stating she is trying to obtain answers from the council officers (Appendix 88)

110) Richard Connaughton and myself met with my Ward Councillors 8th. September 2014. They listened to a recording made of recent events and assured us that they would be speaking to officers of the council.

Nadine Dorries MP visited me at my home with her aide William Joce, we discussed the situation at length and they both listened to the recording we had made of recent events. See, transcript of the recording (Appendix 89). At the end of our discussion Nadine Dorries stated *"Alan., it is all about money, the council know that they have done wrong. they know that they have to admit it, and they know they have to pay compensation"*. She assured me she would make further enquiries with the council. I have sent a copy of the recording and a transcript of it in an "Informative Document" to many people.

An article appeared in the local newspaper (Beds on Sunday) 14th. September 2014 stating that the council had wasted three days of the courts time, by withdrawing its application (Appendix 90).

I also received an E.mail from Nadine Dorries MP stating that the response to her request to the Council for answers are not clear, and has asked for clarification. I have sent her a letter in response. (Appendix 92).

111) I attended a 3-day Public Inquiry in Somerset in support of a fellow Rights of Way sufferer. I was surprised to

see Mr. Maciejwski of Central Beds. council who also attended.

I cannot understand the reason for him attending an Inquiry in Somerset; I can only assume he must have been made aware that I was attending (Through the Inspectorate). his friend, Jean McEntee who was also present at the Inquiry. It seems that the Council are prepared to spend public funds on sending one of their officers to attend a 3-day Inquiry when it does not concern Bedfordshire.

112) The Parish Council sent me a copy of a letter they had received from the Council dated 28th. October 2014 in response to the letter they sent 4th. September 2014. (Appendix 93) the letter stated that the reason they had withdrawn the Section 116 application from the Court was because they were not prepared to spend Public Funds on what they consider a pointless court hearing.

I attended the Parish Council Meeting on 3rd.Noveber 2014 and presented a report to them explaining the situation to date. (Appendix 94) The members were very supportive and were disgusted at the actions of the council. They have sent a letter to the council in response to the letter they had received 28th. October 2014. (Appendix 95).

There are still many documents in my files if required.

....

If you read and consider all the evidence, I am making available to you; and you consider the situation in a fair and impartial manner I fail to see how you cannot be aware of the

Maladministration and Malfeasance which exists within certain sections of Central Bedfordshire Council.

In conclusion! There is a very old saying *"There are none so blind as those that will not see". This saying is derived from (Jeremiah 5:21) "Hear now this, O foolish people, and without understanding: which have eyes, and see not: which have ears, and hear not".* Although this is an old saying, I believe this applies to the present situation.

"The scales of justice are in your hands"

....

NOTE!

This witness statement was prepared for a Public Inquiry which was due to be held
21st-22nd January 2015. However after weeks of preparation (statements etc.) also travel and accommodation being arranged; the Inspectorate informed me by E.mail 4.30pm. Friday 16th. January 2015, that the Inquiry had been CANCELLED. The reason they gave was due "To personal circumstances the Inspector was unable to attend the Inquiry". (Appendix 96) I immediately informed many people who had made arrangements to attend the Inquiry. Most were able to cancel their arrangements in time. However, because some had paid in advance, they were unable to receive a refund. I contacted the Inspectorate (Caroline Baylis) as soon as possible on the morning of Monday 19th. January 2015 asking for more details concerning the very late cancellation. I was informed that it was "Personal" and would give no further information. I received an E.mail from Ms.Baylis 13.30 19th. January 2015 with a letter attached (Appendix 97). The letter attached was

dated 7th. February 2015 and stated, *"May I assure you that as soon as we have spoken to the Inspector you will be contacted about arranging a new date. I would be grateful if you would let me know any dates that you are not available in the next 9 months"*.

I did not receive any communication from CBC regarding the cancellation.

113) I contacted Caroline Baylis 23rd. January 2015 enquiring about the present situation. She refused to inform me of any updates, only to say that because of personal circumstances the Inspectorate were unable to contact the Inspector concerned (Alison Lea). I asked if she could be more specific, but she was not very helpful and stated that she could not inform me any further.

I again contacted Ms. Baylis on the morning of 11th. February 2015, requesting an update on the postponed Public Inquiry., she informed me that she had not heard from the Inspector (Alison Lea) and was unable to give me further information. However, I received an E.mail from Ms. Baylis 12.48 the same day informing me that she had just heard from Alison Lea and that a new Inquiry would be arranged for Mid-September 2015. (Appendix 98)

114) I attended a Public Inquiry in Suffolk 3rd. March 2015. FPS/V3500/14A/2. The Inquiry was concerning a Non-Statutory Schedule 14 Appeal under Section 53 Wildlife & Countryside Act.

The Inquiry was presided over by an Inspector Alan Beckett. The Inquiry commenced in the normal way. However, after a few hours it became apparent that the Inspector was biased in favour of the opponents to the appeal as I have witnessed on other occasions. (See letter to Quality Assurance). Dated 9th. March 2015 (Appendix 99).

115) I received an E.mail from Nadine Dorries MP office 17th. March 2015. (Appendix100). Informing me that Nadine had been in contact with the Inspectorate regarding my situation which stated **"They did not shed any light at all other than to give an overly-bureaucratic explanation that would shame an organisation outside the public sector"**. It went onto say that they were glad to hear of the support by the elected members within the constraints put on them by unelected officials.

116) I received a letter from Caroline Bayliss (Inspectorate) (Appendix 101) informing me that a three day Non-Statutory Public Inquiry would take place 15th.September 2015.

117) 16th. April 2015, I received the usual negative response from Quality Assurance Team (PINS) to a letter I sent to them 9th. March 2015. (Appendix 102).

118) I wrote to ICO 1st. May 2015 requesting them to investigate what I and many others consider a breach of the Data Protection Act. Concerning Mr Alan Beckett (Inspector) and other officers within the Inspectorate concerning their actions which took place at a Public Inquiry 3rd. March 2015. (Appendix 103).

119) I received an E.mail. 6th. May 2015 (Appendix 104) from The Quality Assurance Team (PINS), informing me that, due to a back log of complaints they cannot investigate my request for some time.

120) I received E.mail from SoS DEFRA 29th.May requesting more documents in response to a letter I sent 18th. May. (Appendix 105)

121) I received a letter from Chris Upjohn (LGO) 5th. June 2015 informing me that they will not reinvestigate my Case against CBC and they have closed the complaint and will take no further action. (Appendix 106).

122) I received a letter from Caroline Bayliss (Inspectorate) 22nd. June 2015 informing me that Alison Lea will be unable to attend the Inquiry in September and she will be replaced by Mr. Peter Millman (Appendix 107). I contacted Ms. Bayliss 12.10pm 29th. June, requesting the reason why Ms.Lea had been replaced. She informed me that it was for personal reasons. NOTE! This is the same reason they gave for cancelling the Inquiry in January 2015. I informed Ms. Bayliss that I had evidence that Ms. Lea was conducting site visits and working on a case in February and April. She again informed me that it was personal. (This is not a reason; it is an excuse). I also informed Ms, Baylis that I intend to arrange for the 3-day Inquiry to be filmed and recorded.

123) I received a letter 23rd. June 2015 from Sarah Hill (DEFRA) Customer Contact Unit). (Appendix 108). This letter was in response to several letters I had sent to Liz Truss (SoS DEFRA).

The letter stated. Quote! **"As this route is subject of an upcoming Inquiry, I am afraid it would be inappropriate for the Secretary of State to comment**

or meet to discuss it". (A typical nonsensical response).
I have responded to the letter. [See my letter dated 2nd.
July 2015 (Appendix 109)

124) I received a letter from Caroline Baylis (Inspectorate) 30th. June 2015 informing me that Alison Lea has had to take extended leave. (Appendix 110)

125) After many E.mails to, and from Chairman and some members of DMC it was confirmed 21st. July 2015; that the officials of CBC did not consult or inform the DMC of their desperate action of withdrawing the Section 116 applications from the Magistrates Court on 2nd. September 2014 (Appendix 111). This first notification of their action was not communicated to the DMC until 22nd. September 2014. In the form of an E.mail containing a copy of an E.mail sent to " Beds. On Sunday"

126) A document entitled "The Bowers Case II" has been submitted to the Inspectorate, as evidence to be considered at the Public Inquiry Due to be held 15th,16th. 17th, September 2015.

Alan Bowers
Ein-Ty, 123b Clophill Rd. Maulden Beds.MK45 2AE
Tel 01525 860030
E.mail: bowers-alan@sky.com.

DETAILS OF APPENDIX

Appendix

17/ Threatening letter from Kate Ashbrook (Open Spaces Society) to Mr. Brawn (Beds. County Council).

19/ Letter from Local Government Ombudsman stating they will not investigate to Actions of Beds. County Council.

20/ Letters from Maulden Parish Council and nearly 200 members of the public to the actions of Beds. County Council regarding Footpath 28.

21/ Letter from Beds. County Council acknowledging my application to extinguish Maulden Footpath 28, they state it will not be processed for 12-18 months. Also, a letter to CEO Bedfordshire Council.

22/ Article in Sunday Telegraph referring to actions of Beds. County Council

23/ Letter to Andrea Hill CEO Beds. County Council

24/ Letter from Sally Wileman making false statements

25/ Threating letters from Beds. County Council to Maulden Parish Council and Mid. Beds. District Council regarding Footpath 28.

26/ Letter and E.mail from Mid. Beds. District Council withdrawing they support.

27/ Letter from Mr. Tim Maylyn for CEO stating they have nothing further to say.

28/ Letter to LGO and Planning Inspectorate

29/ Letter from Brawn and E.mail from Nigel Bennett regarding application to Extinguish Footpath 28.

30/ Copy of Minutes of meeting held 21st. August with Mr. McNally regarding Footpath28, and other letter relating to situation.

31/ Letter from Maciejeski regarding gate being erected wrong end of Footpath 28.

32/ Request to Council for minutes and their response

33/ Letter from Nadine Dorries MP

34/ Letter from Central Beds. and others regarding events which took place at D.M.C Meeting which took place 13th. Sept. 2013.

35/ Letter dated 9th. April 2013 from Mr. Maciejewski.

36/ E.mail from Central Beds. stating that original minutes taken at Committee Meeting
13th. February 2013 were destroyed.

37/ Letter from Emerton (Central Beds. Solicitor) stating that the Committee did not
decide that work to be carried out on Bridleway should not be paid for by
Mr. Bowers.

38/ Letter from Planning Inspectorate regarding appeal against Central Beds. Council.

39/ Letter sent to Mr. Tebbut by Central Beds. Council regarding work to be carried
out on Bridleway.

40/ Public Notice issued by Central Beds. Council to Extinguish Footpath 28. 23/5/2013.

41/ Document named ABUSE OF PUBLIC OFFICE issued by Mr. R. Connaughton,

42/ Letter written to CEO Central Beds. informing him of events and actions of
certain officers under his responsibilities.

43/ Order issued to Magistrates Court by Central Beds. 13th. June 2013 to stop-up
Footpath 28.

44/ A confidential letter from Mr. Connaughton to CEO (Central Beds) including
statement by Detective Sargent Steve Broardhust of Dorset Police.

45/ Letter from Richard Carr (CEO Central Beds) dated 3rd. July 2013 in response to
letters previously sent to him 3rd. and 1st. June 2013.

46/ Letter in response to letter from CEO (Central Beds.) 4th. July 2013.

47/ Notice from Magistrates Court to Central Beds. informing them of new hearing.

48/ E.mail from Adam (Maciejewski) to Jean (Inspectorate) making unfounded
Remarks about Mr. Bowers.

49/ Letter from Emerton (Solicitor) on behalf of CEO.

50/ Letter dated 27th. August 2013 from Council Solicitor (Mr.Emerton) in response to letter sent to Mr. Carr CEO (Central Beds) 4th. July 2013. Also, letter dated 28th.

October 2013 to Mr. Connaughton from M r. Atkinson (Head of Legal & Democratic Services (Central Beds.)

51/ Letter from Lucy Derilo (Customer Relations and Information Officer, Central Beds.) Regarding complaint about actions of certain officers within the Council.

52/ E.mail from Mr. Maciejewski try to explain missing documents.

53/ Notice from Magistrates Court to Central Beds. regarding new Court Hearing.

54/54a Letter to CEO insisting meeting, and response.

55/ Statement called THE BOWERS CASE issued to CEO (Central Beds)

56/ Letter to Mr. Carr CEO (Central Beds)

57/ Letter from Mr. Sinclair (Information Governance Manager Central Beds) In response to a request under Freedom of Information Act. In the letter they indicate that they consider me VEXATIOUS because of my frequent questions and requests for information.

58/ Letters to and from Mr. Connaughton and Mr. Carr (CEO)

59/ Detailed letter from Mr. Connaughton to Mr. Carr 7th. March 2014.

60/ Letters to Melaine Clay(Chief Legal and Democratic Service Officer) and E.mails from Sally Wileman (Service Development Manager)

61/ Letter dated 22nd March 2014 to Melanie Clay (ChiefLegal & Democratic Services)

62/ Letter from Melanie Clay dated 25th, April 2014. Although letter is signed by Melanie Clay it is believed to have been written by Sally Wileman.

63/ Email from Sally Wileman

64/ Letter to Melanie Clay from Richard Connaughton dated 29th. May 2014.

65/   Letter to James Jameson (Councillor) from Mr. Connaughton dated 25th. May 2014

66/   Statement by Nadine Dorries

67/   Local Inquiry Statement by Mr. Bowers

68/   Letter to Melanie Clay

69/   Decision by Government Inspector Martin Elliot (Former Rights of Way officer

70/   E.mail to Melanie Clay.

71/   E.mails to and from Mr.Sutton (Council Solicitor)

72/   E.mail to Alxis Crossland (PA to Melanie Clay)

73/   E.mail from Sally Wileman.

74/   E.mail to Mr. Sutton (Council Solicitor)

75/   E.mails to and from Sally Wileman.

76/   Letter from Sally Wileman.

77/   Letter to Luton Magistrates Court

78/79/80/ 81/ letters and E.mail from Luton Magistrates Couut and Sally Wileman.

82/   E.mail. Maciejewski to Sutton stating my Masonic connections.

83/   E.mail to and from Sutton and Maciejewski.

84/   E.mails to and from Mr. Bowers and Sally Wileman.

85/   E.mail from Sally Wileman

86/   E.mail to and from Sutton and Maciejewski.

87/   Letter from Parish Council to CEO Central Beds.

88/   E.mails to and from Mr. Bowers and Nadine Dorries MP

89/   Transcript of Statement on Disc.

90/   Article in Bedford on Sunday

92   E.mail to and from Nadine Dorries MP.

93/   Letter to Parish Council from Melanie Clay.

94   Report to Parish Council.

95   Response from Parish Council to Melanie Clay.

96/   E.mail from Planning Inspctorate.

97/   E.mail and letter from Inspectorate (Caroline Baylis)

98/   E.mail from Inspectorate.

99/   Letter to Planning Inspectorate

100/   E.mail from Nadine Dorries office.

101/   E.mail from Inspectorate.

102,   E.mail letter from Inspectorate

103/   Letter to ICO. (Complaint about Pubic Inquiry in Suffolk)

104/   E.mail response from Customer Quality Assurance (Planning Inspectorate)

105/   **E.mail from CCU. And letter to Local Government Association.**

106/   **Letter from Local Government Ombudsman stating they will not investigate**
          Central Beds. Council. And will enter into any future correspondence Also
          confusing letter from Local Government Association.

107/   **E.mail from Inspectorate referring to forthcoming Public Inquiry.**

108/   **Letter from Defra (customer Support Unit).**

109/   **Response to DEFRA dated 2nd. July 2015.**

110/   **Letter from Planning Inspectorate referring to forthcoming Public Inquiry.**

Also to relevant letters referring to my Witness Statement to be presented at Public Inquiry.

NOTE!

All documents referred to in APPENDIX can be found in Separate file.

How I was "DENIED JUSTICE".
by
Mr. Peter Millman, a Government Inspector directed by DEFRA, and others associated with the Judicial System.

....

Mr. Peter Millman is a Government Inspector who presided over a "Quasi-Judicial" Public Inquiry concerning a "Rights of Way" issue in Bedfordshire, September 2015.

(The whole Inquiry was Videoed and recorded)

It should be noted that: Mr. Millman was formally a "Rights of Way Officer" for a Local Authority. He is not a Solicitor or Barrister!

Note! Mr. Millman was conducting the Inquiry because, a previous decision by a Government Inspector Mr. Mark Yates who carried out an Inquiry in September 2013 was quashed because he refused to consider all evidence made available to him.

....

DETAILS of NON-STUTORY PUBLIC INQUIRY
SEPTEMBER 2015.

At the very beginning of the Inquiry Mr. Millman informed the many members of the public who attended the Inquiry that he would not allow Mr. Alan Bowers (principle objector) to read (present) his opening or witness statement because, *"it was too long and most of its contents was irrelevant to the case".* There were many objections to his actions from people attending the Inquiry. However, he insisted that the statements prepared by Mr. Bowers could not be read out. He then informed the people that had objected that, he and the Council were in procession of the documents and he would consider them as read.

A member of the public informed the Inspector that it was a "Non-statutory Inquiry" and all evidence should be considered. The Inspector (against statutory requirements) refused to have the statements read out. It appeared that Mr. Millman made the rules up to suit himself.

The filmed recording of the Inquiry shows periods of irritation and frustration on the part of Mr. Millman. The film also reveals that Mr. Millman was prepared to LIE and showed BIAS towards the Council and its supporters.

The Inquiry was supposed to be a 3-day Inquiry. But, because, the Inspector refused to allow all evidence to be presented he concluded the Inquiry during the second day.

In his decision letter dated 2nd. October 2015 the Inspector refused the Appeal.

The decision letter of Inspector Millman was compared with actual facts and statements contained within the Filmed version of the Inquiry. It revealed how the Inspector LIED, and DENIED very relevant evidence to be presented and discussed.

It was because of the lack of evidence being considered that the previous Public Inquiry decision was QHASHED!

A legal opinion reveals that:

"Failing to allow you to present your opening statement and witness statement is grounds to judicially review the decision made at the Inquiry as you were not allowed fair procedures in accordance with the Human Rights Act. and article 6 of the European Convention on Human Rights. The

Inquiry can validly exclude evidence and Rule 10 gives them this power. However, they cannot do it to exclude the evidence of the party affected by the Right of Way. This gives rise to a Judicial Review as it does not accord with the guarantee of fair procedures in decision making. You have the right to be heard and it has been violated here".

....

THE PATH TO JUDICIAL REVIEW
SUMMARY OF EVENTS REGARDING

APPLICATION FOR JUDICIAL REVIEW
HISTORY
Treasury Solicitor (TSol). Government Legal Dept GLD)

I wrote a Pre-action Protocol letter to TSol. 30th. November 2015; the following is a summary of events regarding that letter.

1) 22nd. December 2015; I attended Administrative Office (Royal Courts of Justice) and stood in queue for 4 hours to submit application and have it sealed. I was advised the application was being made too late, and that the time to make application had expired. I explained time to submit application did not expire until 2nd. January 2016. However, I was told I must complete Section 8 of form (requesting more time) before my application could be considered.

After application had been sealed, I attended Treasury Solicitors Office, Kemble St. to serve application. I spoke to Prachi Kanse who was surprised that I had made the application before receiving a response to my Pre-action letter dated 30th. November 2015. She asked me to wait; I waited for about 20 minutes and then she issued me with a letter responding to my letter dated 30th. November 2015. The letter she gave me was dated 22nd. December 2015. I therefore assumed she had just written the letter. (*It appears I made the correct decision to visit the Court to avoid my application from being out of time*)

2) 23rd.December 2015, I sent an E.mail and recorded delivery letter to Administrative court explaining my experience at the court the previous day. Also, that I had been advised incorrectly, regarding the time scale for my application. (**No acknowledgement or response**)

3) 8th. January 2016, received a report from Tim Buley (Barrister). The report was sent via. TSol.

Response to report was sent 9th. January 2016 in the form of a letter by Mr. R.ichard Connaughton. (**No acknowledgement or response**).

NOTE! Additional letters sent 9th February, 8th. March 2016.

4) 25th. February 2016, received letter from GLD requesting payment of costs and enclosing a court order by Mrs. Justice Lang, dated 21st. January 2016. The order required a response within 14 days. (4th. February 2016) Note! Order not received until 25th. February 2016, 21days after expiry of date to

respond. A response was sent to GLD 8th. March 2016 **(No acknowledgement or response).**

A request was made by me to my solicitor to arrange a conference with a Barrister to discuss situation. Note! Solicitor did not arrange any conference.

5) 24th. March 2016, received letter from GLD informing me that they had issued a letter to the Administrative Court informing them that they had made an error in the Court Order issued by Mrs. Justice Lang dated 21st. January 2016.

6) 6th. April 2016 a letter to the Court was issued by Woodfines (Solicitors) informing them of the fundamental mistake made by Mrs. Justice Lang regarding the Court Order issued 21st. January 2016.

7) 25th. April 2016, the Court responded to Woodfines (Solicitor) stating that the case had been referred back to Mrs. Justice Lang for further consideration.

8) 5th. May 2016, I sent a very long and comprehensive letter, including many informative documents (Evidence) to Mr. Martyne Cowlin (Admin Court). Note! the letter was sent recorded delivery. **(No acknowledgment or response)**

9) Friday 13th. May 2016, I received an E.mail from Woodfines(Solicitor) informing me that an order had been issued by Mrs. Justice Lang dated 9th. May 2016. The order stated that I had 14 days to respond from 12th May 2016. (26th. May 2016).

10) Monday 16th. May 2016, I tried to contact Woodfines(Solicitor) to request them to respond to the order and was told the solicitor (Catherine Sandbach) was not available. I tried again everyday up to Friday 20th. May 2016 and was informed that the solicitor was not available. After insisting I spoke to someone, I spoke to Keith Jones (Partner) who informed me that the solicitor (Catherine Sandbach) had been withdrawn from my case, no reason was given.

11) Because of the time scale, I Emailed and wrote to the Administrative Court 24th. May 2016. (Letter sent recorded delivery) requesting further time to respond to the order dated 9th. May 2016. **(No acknowledgement or response).**

12) I sent an E.mail to Woodfines(Solicitor) informing them of my dissatisfaction regarding the way my case was being conducted. I received an E.mail in response requesting me to inform the court that they no longer represent me. I tried to contact Keith Jones but was informed that he was not available. I sent an Email. Requesting them to inform me when and why, Catherine Sandbach was withdrawn from my case. **(No acknowledgement or response).**

13) Because I had not received a response to my letter to the Court dated 24th. May 2016, I contacted the Post Office to see if my letter had been received, I was advised to contact the court. I telephoned the Administrative Court Office at 11.20am. 2nd. June 2016. After a very long wait I eventually spoke to a lady called Dorothy, she informed me that they had received my letter. I asked if she could read the contents of the letter to me; she requested me to stay on the line. I waited until 11.36am. when the line went dead. I redialled the number and again after a very long wait I made contact with Dorothy, she apologised and transferred me to the Case Progression Team, I eventually spoke to a lady called Momotaj. We had a long conversation and she eventually informed me that my case had been closed.

She also informed me that the court had sent an E.mail to Woodfine(Solicitors) on 26th. May 2016. (This Email had not been forwarded to me.). She kindly Emailed me a copy of the E.mail. Because I was very confused by the whole process, she informed me that I should make an application for the case to be renewed. She advised me that I should complete Form N244 and sent it with a cheque for £255.

14) I received a letter from the court dated 1st. June 2016 informing me that my case had been closed.

15) 5th. June 2016, I sent a letter (Sent special delivery) (Received and signed for 8.11am. 7th.June 2016). My letter was addressed to Administrative Court. Explaining my concern about the manner in which my case is being conducted. I included 20 letters to confirm the information contained in my letter. **(No acknowledgement or response)**

16) Letter sent to court 27th. June 2016, (special delivery) requesting information regarding previous letters and E.mails. **(No acknowledgement or response).**

17) E.mail sent to Admin Court. 25th. July 2016, requesting response to communications.
(No acknowledgement or response)

18) I received a letter from Kimberlie Eatough (Admin. Team Leader). 3rd. August 2016.

19) I responded to Kimberlie Eatough 8th. August 2016. Letter and documents received and signed for 7.45am. 9th. August 2016. (By Jordon)

20) Letter received from GLD. 15th. August 2016. requesting payment of costs. Letter from Richard Hilton.

21) Letter sent to Prachi Kanse GLD. from Richard Connaughton dated 16th. August 2016.
(No acknowledgement or response)

22) Mr. Connaughton sent a letter by E.mail to Ms. Kanse, 25th. August 2016.

23) I received a response to my letter dated 8th. August 2016. The letter dated 30th. August 2016 was a very evasive letter from Geraint Evans (GLD). Informing me; that if I was not satisfied with the way my complaint has been dealt with. I should write to Communications and Customer Services Team.

24) I have written to Communications and Customer Service Team, informing them of my dissatisfaction at the manner in which my case has been conducted from the beginning, and have supplied them with many documents to support my complaint. 8th. September 2015.

Letter sent special delivery 10.19am 9th. September 2016. It was received and signed for by Peter 11.27am. 12th. September 2016. **(no acknowledgement or response)**

25) Mr. Connaughton wrote to Prachi Kanse 15th. September 2016 referring to the 5 grounds which they consider "Unarguable and without merit". **(no acknowledgement or response)**

26) I again wrote to Communications and Customer Service Team Services Team (CCST) 29th. September 2016 enclosing document "J'accuse" and letter to GLD. (Sent special deliver)
(no acknowledgement or response)

27) I received a typical evasive letter from Richard Redgrave (CCST) 30th. September 2016.

28) I responded to Mr. Redgrave's letter 13th. October2016. I commented on various points he had stated in his letter (30th. September 2016)

29) Richard wrote a series of letters and Emails to Mr. Lee John-Charles head of Litigation Legal Dept. GLD. 1st, 4th, 8th,9th,11th. November 2016. **(no acknowledgement or response)**

30) Richard wrote further letters to Lee John-Charles 21st. Nov 2016 and 7th. December 2016
(no acknowledgement or response)

31) HMCTS supplied incorrect information to Parliamentary Ombudsman regarding my case.

(Letter dated 22nd. December 2016 from Parliamentary Ombudsman, received 27th. December 2016. Letter stated "we have decided to take no further action"

32) Because of the Christmas period it was not possible to communicate with anyone. I eventually sent an Email. to Ms. Wright (PHSO) 3rd. January 2017 explaining that the Courts and the Inspectorate had supplied them with incorrect information.

33) Richard Connaughton wrote a long informative letter to Ms. Wright (PHSO) 4th. January 2017, referring to the incorrect information they had received from Courts and Inspectorate. I again sent an Email. 6th. January 2017. **(no acknowledgement or response)**

34) I received an Email from Ms.Wright (PHSO) informing me that she was on maternity leave and would not be responding to any communications.

35) I wrote a long informative letter to Ms. Wright (PHSO) dated 11th. January 2017. Because I had been communicating with her previously.

36) I wrote to Mr. Redgrave (HM Courts) 14th. January 2017 requesting him to respond, to various communications/correspondence, between us over the past weeks.

37) I received a letter from Mr. Redgrave (HM Courts) 18th. January 2017. The letter was dated 12th. January 2017. The letter informed me that "I do not propose to comment further if you write again on this matter".

And suggested I contact my MP to refer my case to Parliamentary Ombudsman (Which I have already done)

38) I wrote a letter to PHSO 23rd. January 2017 addressed to Sir/Madam because I had not been informed who had replaced Ms. Wright. I also wrote to Nadine Dorries to keep her up to date with the situation.

39) Mr. Connaughton wrote to Mr. Redgrave (HM.Courts) 25th. January 2017 informing him of his dissatisfaction at the treatment I had received from HM Courts and Tribunal Service
   (No acknowledgement or response.)

40) I again wrote to PHSO 26th. January 2017 enclosing the letter written by Mr. Connaughton.

41) I contacted PHSO 3rd. February 2017 and spoke to Alec Fox who informed me that there was nothing further they could do. I eventually spoke to a lady called Janet in Customer Care who was most helpful. She advised me to complete certain forms which she would send to me to have my case reviewed. She phoned me later that day to inform me that her manager had looked at my case and it would be reviewed without completing any forms.

42) I received an Enforcement order from Andrew Wilson & Co. High Court Enforcement. Dated 10th. February 2017. Relating to an order, issued by the High Court 21st. January 2016. I wrote to Andrew Wilson & Co. explaining that the order issued 21st. January 2016 giving me 14 days to respond, was not made available to me until 24th. February 2016

Therefore I was unable to contest it. The same Judge issued another Order dated 9ᵗʰ. May 2016 quashing the previous order because mistakes were made by the court and stated "costs reserved". I also contacted Richard Hilton (GLD) to discuss the situation. After a while he said "I am not prepared to spend any more time discussing this case" and put the phone down.

43) Mr. Connaughton sent an Email to Prachi Kanse (GLD) 17ᵗʰ. February 2017. Regarding the enforcement order. I also wrote a letter to Mr. Lee John-Charles (GLD) 17ᵗʰ. February 2017 informing him of the situation and requested him to investigate my case.
(No acknowledgement or response)

44) I contacted PHSO 20ᵗʰ. February 2017 and spoke to Phil Whitehead who informed me that my case is now being investigated by Mr. Mark Hair. I wrote to PHSO 24ᵗʰ. February 2017 informing them of what I had been advised.

45) Mr. Connaughton sent an Email to Mr. John-Charles (GLD) 24ᵗʰ. February 2017 informing him of the situation, and that it was a case of "Misconduct in Public Office" which should be considered by the Metropolitan Police. He stated he was tired of the lawlessness and allowed 14 days to do what is right.
(No acknowledgement or response)

46) I was visited by an Enforcement Officer 3ʳᵈ. March 2017 relating to the Enforcement order issued 13ᵗʰ. February 2017. I had no choice but to pay him. I made him aware of the situation and he advised me to contact the court and appeal.

47) I hand delivered a letter and evidence to the Bedford County Court 16th. March 2017 requesting "Judgement to be Set Aside" and "Stay of Writ".

48) I received a response to my letter on 17th. March 2017, requesting me to comment on the contents of the letter.

49) I hand delivered a letter to the Bedford County Court, 22nd. March 2017. The letter also contained various other documents to be considered.

50) Letter to Mr. Lee John-Charles (GLD) 24th. April 2017, including request for costs.
(No acknowledgement or response).

51) Sent a letter to Prachi Kanse (GLD) 29th. April 2017, informing her of an incident concerning the mental state of my wife., caused by the actions of GLD. Received a response by Email. 3rd. May 2017 stating she would respond as soon as possible.

52) I received a letter from Bedford Court 6th. May 2017, informing me that "The County Court can do nothing. It is a High Court matter. They also enclosed all the documents I had supplied them with. So now I have to apply to the High Court.

53) 8th. May 2017, I telephoned High Court for information. I spoke to a lady who was most helpful, and she said she would send me a pack which would explain everything I need to do.

54) 9th. May 2017, I received a large bundle from Civil Appeal Office as promised. I read contents, and because it is very complicated, I intend to attend RCJ to ask for assistance in completing the necessary forms to make my claim.

55) Contacted RCJ and made appointment to attend Personal Support Unit (PSU) at 11.30am. Tuesday 16th. May

56) Tuesday 16th. May 2017. I attended PSU at Royal Court. The following is a summary of my experience at Royal Courts of Justice.

ROYAL COURTS OF JUSTICE EXPERIENCE

On 16th. March 2017, I attended Bedford County Court to deliver an application to have a court order judgement issued January 2016 to be "Set aside". I received a letter from the court dated 17th. March 2017, requesting more information. The information was hand delivered to the court 22nd. March 2017. I received a letter from the court. 6th. May 2017 informing me that they could not help, and I should apply to the High Court.

I contacted the High Court 8th. May 2017 and spoke to a lady who was very pleasant and helpful. She informed me that I need to make an application using various forms. She kindly mailed the forms and guidance to me the next day. The forms appeared quite complicated. I contacted the High Court again, and was referred to the Personal Support Unit (PSU).

I arranged a meeting with PSU for 11.30am. Tuesday16th. May 2017.

I travelled to Royal Courts of Justice, London, to attend the meeting. I was seen by a very pleasant and helpful lady named Hannah. We spent one and a half hours together where she advised me how to complete the forms and application. She advised me to go to the Fees Office to obtain an Exemption Certificate using form EX160. I attended the fees office in another part of the building and was issued with an Exemption Certificate. The people there were very helpful, and suggested I attend the Appeals Office in another part of the building to see if the Certificate was adequate for my purpose. The people at the Appeals Office who attended to me did not appear to understand what I required, and a senior officer directed me to "The Admin Office" in another part of the building. The girl who attended to me at the Admin. Office did not appear to know what I required; I supplied her with all the papers. Eventually she informed me that she would get a more senior person to attend to me. After some time, another person attended to me. I understand the person was a "Case progression Officer". This person appeared very officious, and when I tried to explain the situation, she became very bureaucratic and attempted to talk over me. She appeared to be reluctant to listen, and understand what I was trying to explain to her. I realised I was not going to receive any assistance from her. I asked for her name; she said "why!". I said I need to know her name for my records, she reluctantly wrote her name on a scrap of paper. Because it was not very legible, I asked if she could spell it out for me. She said "We do not usually give out names".

I was quite frustrated and informed her that whenever I write to the Royal Courts Admin Office, I never receive any acknowledgement or response. She stated "We do not respond to letters".

It became obvious she wanted to end our conversation and wished to pull down the blind at the counter. I read the name she had written on the piece of paper and believe it read "Clodeagh O'Neill, Case Progression Office, Administrative Court."

I had travelled to Royal Courts of Justice in London, to seek assistance and advice; I spent three and a half hours going from one department to another. I have to say; most of the people I dealt with were courteous and helpful, however I was disappointed and frustrated at the service I received at the Administrative Office.

I am 78 years old, and do not enjoy travelling to London to seek assistance and advice. However, I felt I needed assistance, but, was disappointed at the way I was treated by Ms. O,Neill.

....

57) 18th. May 2017 sent Email to Cloagh O'Neill (Admin office)

58) 25th. May 2017 sent bundle to Civil Appeals Office regarding application for Judicial Review, including 3 copies of: N161 forms, Copies of Court orders, Remission Certificate, Summary of Events, Letter to Lee John-Charles9GLD), Royal Courts of Justice experience and E.mails to Ms.O'Neill.

59) 6th. June 2017, I received a letter from Mr. John Hebden (Registry Office) HMCTS. returning all the documents I had sent to the Court 25th. May 2017. I telephoned Mr. Hebden and asked him to explain the contents of his letter. I explained the situation and informed him of the information and advice I had received from the Administrative Court Office. He informed me that I had been given incorrect information and advised me to contact Admin. Office. Tel No. 02079476655

I telephoned Admin. Office and spoke to a very pleasant and helpful lady called Karen Welford. We had a long conversation and I explained the situation. She informed me that I had been misinformed by the Admin Office regarding the required forms to make an application. She explained that I need to make a new application using form N244 together with a completed EX160 form regarding fees. She advised me to complete the forms and send them with a letter explaining my situation, for her attention to Administrative Court Office, Royal Courts of Justice, Strand, London, WC2A 2LL. She also advised me that if I wished to make a complaint, I should write to Sana Gilani her office manager.

60) 10th. June 2017, Sent letter to Karen Wellford (RCJ) and included completed forms N244 and EX160 and various documents to support my Application Notice.

61) Note; I sent a letter to Prachi Kanse 29/4/17. Received E.mail response 3/5/17 stating "Will respond as soon as possible". Sent Email 2/6/17 asking for response. Received E.mail response 8/6/17, stating "I hope to respond shortly". Sent another E.mail 14/6/17 asking "How long do you require to respond?"

62) Received letter from Admin Court dated 16th. June 2017 including sealed application using form N244.

63) 20th. June 2017 served sealed application on CBC and GLD.

64) 21st. June 2017, Received an Email response from Prachi Kanse in response to my letter dated 24th. April 2017 and subsequent follow up Emails.

65) Sent letter and enclosed letter to Karen Wellford (Admin Court) 24th. June 2017.

66) 9th. July 2017, I sent letter and information to Admin. Court; also letter to Sana Gilani (Office manager) (See below)

IS

JUSTICE

JUST

A

WORD?

BY

A.J.Bowers

"All that is needed for INJUSTICE to triumph is for good and just men, and women to do nothing"

FORWORD:

"Justice is a concept on ethics and law that means that people behave in a way that is fair, equal and balanced for everyone"

....

This is a story about "The Struggle for JUSTICE"

PREFACE

During the early parts of our life we are taught to Respect and Accept many things that will affect us during our lives.

It could be: Religion, Education; Medical; Politics; Laws; etc.

There are of course, many learned and devoted people within these particular subjects who are dedicated, truthful, and sincere.

However, as we progress though life, we discover by experience, that not all is as we expected.

I consider myself to be a normal law-abiding citizen with certain standards which I endeavour to uphold.

Over the past 27 years I have experienced much distress and financial burden attributed to the actions of some, who we would expect to be Truthful, Lawful, and Sincere, whilst acting out the particular positions they hold.

Recently I have produced a book called "The Path & I" which tells in great detail the distress I and my family have experienced through the actions of those who "Derive pleasure at the distress of others "

This document "Justice what Justice" reveals the Malfeasance and Malicious actions of a company of Solicitors in whom I placed my trust to obtain Justice.

NOTE; All documents, files etc. referred to in "Justice what Justice" are available within my files.

Index

Chapter I: Justice what Justice!

Details of attempting to obtain Justice through normal Judicial system available to members of the public.

Chapter II: Action taken against Solicitors!

Details of action taken against Woodfines Solicitors (Bedford) for misconduct and dishonesty by Solicitors Regulation Authority including details of case and disciplinary action by Solicitors Disciplinary Tribunal.

Chapter III: Continuing Struggle to obtain Justice!

Details of attempting to re-open case with Legal Ombudsman using newly found evidence against the actions and Malfeasance of Woodfines Solicitors (Bedford).

CHAPTER: I   Justice what Justice

Because of the malicious and unacceptable actions of Central Bedfordshire Council (CBC), regarding a public Footpath that had been imposed upon my property in 1997 had caused me and my family, many years of distress and financial burden, I sought the advice of a local solicitor (Woodfine's of Bedford).

I wished to enquire into the possibility of referring the actions of CBC to the Courts regarding "Misconduct in Public Office".

I first attended Woodfine's Bedford Office 2nd. July 2014 where I met Catherine Sandbach (Litigation Solicitor). We spent a few hours discussing my case and I produced many documents to illustrate my claim.

I received a letter from Woodfine's dated 18th. July 2014, the letter set out my intentions and was requested to pay £234 for them to investigate my case.

Ms. Sandbach informed me that the details of my claim would be investigated by their Litigation Team to access the strength of my case.

On 3rd. September 2014 I sent an E.mail to Woodfine's informing them of the recent actions of CBC when they withdrew a Section 116 WCA from the court which was due to take place 8th, 9th, 10th. September 2014, at Luton Magistrates Court.

The Section 116, was presented to the Court by CBC. 13th. June 2013. The case was to be heard 17th. July 2013. On the day CBC requested an Adjournment. The case was adjourned until 2nd. January 2014. The CBC attended and requested a 2nd. Adjournment. The case was adjourned until 8th, 9th, 10th. September 2014.

The CBC requested a further adjournment 21st. August 2014. The Court refused their application. In desperation CBC withdrew the Section 116 application from the Court 2nd. September 2014.

After receiving this information, Woodfine's sent me an E.mail 4th. September 2014 stating "It seems to me that their actions could continue to build your potential case for misfeasance in public office in relation to the ongoing actions of the council and its officers".

During September 2014 I delivered more documents and evidence to Woodfine,s.

I received a letter from Ms. Sandbach 4th. November 2014 stating that Woodfine,s are prepared to enter into "Conditional Fee Agreement" (CFA).

I attended their office in Bedford 10th. November 2014 where, we both signed a "Conditional Fee Agreement", I also suppled them with a very detailed dossier relating to "Misconduct in Public Office" to present to their barrister. Ms. Sandbach sounded very positive and indicated the case would be presented to CBC by the end of the year 2014.

I sent an E.mail to Ms. Sandbach 23rd. November attaching a copy of a letter I had sent to the Inspectorate 21st. November 2014 illustrating the Misconduct of CBC and others.

I wrote a letter to Chief Executive, (CBC)14th. February 2015, illustrating the corruption within his authority, and sent a copy to Woodfine,s. (received no acknowledgement).

I made several calls to Woodfine,s enquiring about my case. Each time they apologised for not contacting me. I eventually received an E.mail 1st. April 2015 from Cristopher Northway (Trainee solicitor) stating. *"Catherine is continuing to liaise with the barrister in this matter, and will provide you with a comprehensive update after Easter"*.

I attended the Bedford office 14th. April 2015 where Catherine informed me that she was still waiting for a response from the barrister. While I was there, she endorsed a letter (Signed and stamped) which I had written to the Planning Inspectorate.

I received an E.mail from Catherine Sandbach 1st. May 2015 informing me that she had referred my case to a different barrister, and hoped to have an opinion by Mid. May.

I received an E.mail from Catherine 17th. July 2015 requesting me to supply further information for the barrister to consider. I hand delivered the requested information 20th. May 2015.

Despite many attempts to contact Woodfine,s. I received an E.mail 19th. October 2015 from Catherine informing me of the barrister's opinion regarding my case. (Not very positive). I requested a copy of the barrister's report and received a copy early in November 2015

I attended the Bedford office 23rd. November 2015 and discussed the situation with Catherine. I supplied a letter and a comprehensive dossier which included details and information concerning a public Inquiry which took place September 2015. I also informed Catherine that I would be applying for Judicial Review, and requested they represent me.

I attended the Bedford office 29th. December 2015 and discussed the situation with Catherine and informed her of the present situation regarding my application for Judicial Review. Note: *She did not appear to be au-fait with the procedure.*

I hand delivered a bundle for the attention of Catherine Sandbach to the Bedford office 15th. January 2016.

I met with Catherine 29th. February 2016 to discuss the situation, and agreed to instruct a barrister, and to respond to a letter I had received from the Government Legal

Department (GLD). We also agreed it would be appropriate to have a conference with the barrister.

I sent an E.mail. to Catherine 10th. March 2016 with an attachment (a letter to GLD dated 8th. March 2016). I also requested an update on the proceedings.

I received an E.mail. from Catherine 24th. March 2016 informing me she would be out of the office for the Easter break. She also informed me that the barrister she had contacted would not be available until the latter part of April and asked if I wished to look into another Counsel.

I received an E.mail 4th. April 2016 from Catherine informing me that they propose to send a letter to the Royal Courts of Justice in response to information received from court, which indicated the statement made by the Judge to be incorrect and ask that they reconsider my application for Judicial Review.

I sent an E.mail to Catherine 25th. April 2016 informing her that I had received an E.mail from Prachi Kanse (GLD) informing me that the Judge had made an error in her decision regarding my application for Judicial Review.

I received an E.mail. 27th. April 2016 from Catherine attaching a letter they had received from GLD which stated that the papers had been referred back to the Judge for further consideration.

I received an E.mail. Friday 13th. May 2016 from Sarah Craddock (Legal Secretary Litigation) in the name of Catherine Sandbach with an attachment from the Court granting 14 days in which to renew (review) my application for Judicial Review. She also states *"Accordingly, this would be a goodtime for us to put all of the information together in one place for them to determine whether permission should be allowed. I am forwarding this to the clerks for barrister in order to press them for an urgent conference in light of this so that we can get his input before anything is put together.*

If he is not available within this time, I will ask for an alternative barrister to provide advice.

NOTE: This is the time when things appear to become mysteriously disconnected regarding Catherine Sandbach.

....

WHAT HAPPENED to CATHERINE SANDBACH?

I tried to contact Catherine Sandbach first thing Monday 16th. May 2016, and was told she was not available, and that I would be contacted later. I tried every day up to Friday 20th.2016 and was told she is not available. I insisted that I spoke to someone, and eventually spoke to Keith Jones a Senior Partner of (Woodfine;s Solicitors). Mr. Jones informed me that Catherine Sandbach had been witdrawn from my case. He would not explain why.

I received an E.mail. from Mr. Jones 20th. May 2014 in which he informed me of certain barristers and recommended Kate Oiley. He requested me to phone him Monday 23rd. May 2016.

I telephoned Mr. Jones 23rd. May 2016 in the morning; I expressed my dissatisfaction at the manner in which Woodfine's had conducted my case. I received an E.mail. from Mr. Jones 15:06 23rd. May 2016. Setting out different proposals and requested £5000 before continuing my case.

Because I only had a few days to respond to the court (26th. May 2016), I took it upon myself to respond. I sent a letter by E.mai 11:04 24th. May 2016. I also sent the letter by recorded mail 12:47. I also sent an E.mail 10:18 24th. May 2016 to Mr.

Jones, informing him of my actions and my dissatisfaction at the service I had received from Woodfine's.

I received an E.mail from Sarah Cradock (Woodfine's) 12:08. 24th. May 2016 requesting me to complete an attached form.

The form was to be sent to the Court informing them that Woodfine's no longer acted for me.

I sent an E.mail   26th. May 2016 (12:27) to Mr. Jones informing him that I had tried to contact him, but was told he was not available. I also wished to know Why and When Catherine Sandbach was withdrawn from my case. I also informed him that because of my dissatisfaction with Woodfine's , and because of the time factor I had contacted the Court directly regarding my request for Judicial Review.

NOTE; I had discovered that Catherine Sandbach ceased to be employed by Woodfines (Solicitors). I have enquired when and why she left their employment.

I received a further E.mail 26th. May 2016(12:59) attaching an E.mail they had received from the court (11:22), They also threatened me with costs of £500 if I did not send a copy of the form they had sent me 24th. May 2016. I sent an E.mail in return (17:0) stating that I would send a completed form to the court and GLD as soon as possible.

I informed Mr. Jones 27th. May 2016 that I had sent the completed forms and sent him a copy for his information.

On the same day 26th. May 2016 12:58, Mr. Jones through Ms. Eagle sent an E.mail to the Court attempting to explain the situation. The final paragraph of the E.mail. states *"If the court feels able to declare of its own motion that we are not the claimant's solicitors on the record that would be very helpful in all the circumstances"*

I sent an E.mail to Ms. Eagle(Legal Secretary) 31st. May 2016 requesting that in view of the fact I no longer wished

Woodfine's to represent me, to arrange for me to collect all documents/evidence I had supplied regarding my case.

I received a letter from the Court 1st. June 2016 (From A.Lee Senior Operations Manager) informing me *(Leave to apply for Judicial Review has been refused and notice of that refusal was served upon the claimant on 05/02/2016. No request to reconsider the decision at the hearing has been lodged by the claimant within the period prescribed by the Civil Procedure Rule 54.12(4). Accordingly, I write to inform you that the file in this matter has been closed)*

The information in this letter is untrue and refers to a different appeal?????.

I wrote to the Court 5th June 2016 informing the court of their incorrect information and the Maladministration of Woodfine's (Solicitors). I Stated;

"Because of the confusion and mistakes made by the Court regarding my application for Judicial Review made 22nd. December 2015, and because of the Maladministration of my solicitors (Woodfine's) I find myself in a very difficult and unacceptable position. Therefore, for Justice to be seen to be done. I request that my case be reviewed (not renewed), and all the evidence be reconsidered. I believe I have adhered to the correct procedure; it is because of the mistakes made by the Court and others that we have arrived at the present situation" I also supplied 20 letters/documents for consideration

I received a letter 28th. June 2016 from Mr. Jones (Solicitor) enclosing an Invoice for £6139.20.

I wrote a letter 11th. July 2016 to Mr. Jones again requesting information regarding the reason Catherine Sandbach had been withdrawn from my case; and why I was not informed, despite the many occasions I had tried to contact her. I also informed him that I contested the contents of the Invoice sent to me 28th. June 2016.

I received a response from Mr. Jones 13th. July 2016 endeavouring to answer my questions regarding Catherine Sandbach. He also requested me to pay for the services of Mr. Feldman (Barrister) who they had instructed. He also informed me that they would not release the documents I had requested.

I responded to Mr. Jones 21st. July 2016 and made several comments. I again informed Mr. Jones that because of the action or non-action of their company I had been subjected to much distress and unnecessary action. I also informed him that I had evidence of previous "Professional Misconduct" regarding Woodfine's (Solicitors)

I received a letter 25th. July 2016 from Sarah O'Brian (Trainee legal Executive, Woodfine,s) informing me that Mr. Jones was not available, and it would be inappropriate to address the points raised in my letter dated 22nd. July 2016 (should be 21st. July).

I received a letter 3rd. August 2016 from Mr. Jones attempting to respond to some of my concerns. He also threatened me with further action if I did not respond by 10th. August 2016

I received a letter 17th. August 2016 from Denise Turner (Credit Controller, Woodfine,s) stating the balance of the Invoice could be subject to interest at the rate of 8.5% per. annum.

....

After seeking advice. I was advised to contact The Legal Ombudsman at PO Box 6806, Wolverhampton, WV1 9WJ.

I wrote to The Legal Ombudsman 28th. September 2016; explaining my situation and enclosed many documents. I received a response from Legal Ombudsman 14th. October 2016 supplying me with a Case No. CMP-046872.

I received an Enforcement Notice 13th. January 2017 from an address in Croydon referring to a Court Order issued in Salford (Manchester), and a notice from a Court in Oldham (Lancs). NOTE: I had no knowledge of these orders. These orders were made by Woodfine's relating to an Invoice presented to me June 2016, which I had contested. After many hours on the phone and various investigations, I was advised to present certain forms and letters explaining the true situation. I eventually received an order to attend a hearing at Bedford County Court 14th. February 2017.

I hand delivered a formal Letter of Complaint to Woodfine's, 7th. February 2017 as instructed by The Legal Ombudsman.

I received an E.mail from Claire Potter (Woodfine's) 9th. February 2017 stating that they had considered my case, and agreed to *"Set aside the Judgement against you and to stay the writ of execution"* whilst they consider my complaint letter of 7th. February 2017. She also requested me to sign a Consent Order which she had attached. She added that after the order had been signed, they would file it with the court prior to the hearing 14th. February 2017 so that the hearing could be vacated.

I received a phone call from Woodfine's 6.20pm 9th. February 2017 asking me to sign the form and send it to them. I informed them that I had no intention of signing the form and would be attending the hearing. (they did not appear to be happy with my intentions).

I received a letter dated 10th. February 2017 from Adrian Frost (Client Care Partner) Woodfine's. He stated my Complaints Letter dated 7th. February 2017 had been passed to him. He advised me that he would investigate and get back to me within the timeframe of the firms "Internal Complaints Procedure"

I sent an E.mail to Ms.Potter 12th. February 2017 informing her that I intend to attend the hearing 14th. February and state my case. I received a telephone call early Monday 13th. February 2017 from Mr. Keith Jones (Woodfine's), he informed me that if I signed the form, there would be no need to attend the hearing. I advised him that I had every intention of attending the hearing. He shouted "We will see you in court" and put down the phone.

I attended the Court hearing at Bedford Court Tuesday 14th, February 2017.

See details of my attendance

Could this be the shortest Court Hearing?
Alan Bowers

I was directed by Bedford County Court to attend a Court Hearing at 10.0am Tuesday 14th. February 2017.

I attended the Court at St.Paul's Square Bedford.

I entered the building at 9.55am. And was directed to an office at the rear of the building, which meant I had to leave the building and walk around to the rear of the building to access the office.

After going through security, I presented the order to the court officer at 10.07am.

I was informed that the case had already been held and judgement had been made at 10.0am.

The case was concerning a court order issued by Woodfines (Solicitors) Bedford, against me for £7053.57; which I wished to contest.

The court officer informed me that a representative for Woodfines had attended earlier, and the case had been dealt with.

I requested to see the Judge. The officer accompanied me to a room to see the Judge. I asked the Judge (Judge Ayres) to explain the situation to me. He was very pleasant, and stated. "Woodfines attended earlier and judgement has been made to [set aside judgement and to stay the writ].". I was very confused and asked "How long did it take" he replied "Twenty seconds". I could not understand the situation, and enquired, how could a decision be made without me being present.

He said *"Mr. Bowers do not worry, it has all been sorted, and you will no longer be pursued regarding this matter"*. I had to accept what he stated, but I informed him that I wished to make a counter claim against Woodfines; for the distress and financial burden they had imposed upon me.

He informed me that *"Woodfines and you should get your heads together"*.

NOTE:
Woodfines have been representing me in an attempt to bring an action against Central Bedfordshire Council for Misconduct and Malfeasance. We had a "No Win no Fee" agreement made 10th. November 2014. Also, in my attempt to obtain a Judicial Review, against a decision made by a Government Inspector. Over that period, they have been most unprofessional and did not appear to be familiar with the proceedings. I have requested the Legal Ombudsman to investigate the conduct and actions of Woodfines (Solicitors).

I received another letter from Adrian Frost 16th, February 2017 stating he had investigated the file and requested that I should arrange a meeting with him and Keith Jones regarding my concerns.

I wrote to the Legal Ombudsman 20th. February 2017 informing him of recent events and repeated my request to investigate the conduct and actions of Woodfine's (Solicitors).

I received a Judgement Order from High courts of Justice BEDFIRD 22nd. February 2017 informing me that,
1/ Judgement had been set aside.
2/ Writ had been stayed.
3/ There be no order for costs.

I also received a letter from Land Registry dated. 20th. February 2017, informing me that Woodfine's had cancelled the application to enter a restriction on my property,

I wrote to the Legal Ombudsman 24th. February 2017, informing them of recent events and supplied them with a copy of my "Summary of events concerning Woodfine;s Solicitors"

I wrote to Adrian Frost (Woodfine's) 25th. February 2017 in response to his letter date 16th. February 2017. I informed him that I agree in principle to a meeting with Woodfine's and put various questions to him.

I sent an E.mail to Woodfine's informing them that because I had not received an acknowledgement or response to my letter dated 25th.February 2017, I intend to take further action if I do not receive a response within 3 days.

I received an E.mail from Malcolm Tattersall a freelance journalist. 3rd. March 2017. He had contacted Woodfine,s regarding my case, and asked many questions. Woodfine,s gave a negative response.

See details of questions and answers below!

Details of Questions and answers:

Mr. Tattersall wrote:

Hello,

I am a freelance journalist and have recently been talking to Mr. Alan Bowers, who at one time you were acting for in his legal fight over a disputed footpath, (the now notorious "Footpath 28") across his land in Maulden.

He claims that your firm agreed to take on his case under a Conditional Fee Agreement after telling him he had a strong case, but then suddenly out of the blue sent him a bill for nearly £7000.

Mr. Bowers is quite upset over what he considers rather shabby treatment by your firm. However, of course there are two sides to every story. So, in the interests of fairness, I am contacting you to ask if you would please tell me:

1/ *Why and when was your solicitor Catherine Sandbach, who had been dealing with Mr. Bowers, suddenly withdrawn from the case? Mr. Bowers claims that although he asked for a reason, senior partner Keith Jones would not tell him.*

2/ *When did Ms. Sandbach leave Woodfine's employment? Specifically, was this on or before May 20 2016?*

3/ *Why was Mr. Bowers subsequently sent a bill for £7053.57 when he and Woodfine's had signed a conditional fee agreement?*

4/ *Why did you then apply to a judge in Greater Manchester, some 160 miles away, for a court order against Mr. Bowers?*

5/ *Would it not have been easier, and perhaps more sensible, when all the parties involved were based in Bedfordshire, to apply to the court in Bedford, Luton, or even Milton Keynes?*

6/   Is it also true that Mr. Bowers was not informed in advance of the court hearing so that he was able to argue his case and defend himself?

7/   Why did you then apply to the Land Registry for an interim charge on Mr. Bowers' home in Maulden?

8/   Why if Mr. Bowers really did owe this quite sizeable sum, did Woodfine's then agree to "set aside judgement and stay the writ" against him after he objected in a most vociferous manner and threaten to complain to the Legal Ombudsman about the way he had been treated?

I am sure you would wish to comment on such matters before any article is published, so I would be grateful if you could come back to me asap - even if only, or whatever reason, to say "No comment".

Should you wish to discuss this over the phone or in your office, then please

Get in touch. My mobile number is ....

Thanks,

Malcolm Tattersall.

....

Mr. Jones responded by Email. 2:35 Mar. 3. 2017.

Dear Mr. Tattersall,

Thank you for the below Email, which has been referred to me, since my name is mentioned.

Your query appears to relate to someone whom you believe to be a client of this firm.

As a journalist, you will be doubtless aware that if Mr. Bowers were or had been a client, I would not be permitted by rules of professional conduct to respond to your query.

Kind regards

Keith Jones.

Mr. Tattersall responded 3:17 March 3, 2017.

Thanks Mr. Jones. I will say in my article that you were given the opportunity to respond but replied "No comment"

Mal Tattersall

……………………………………..

I received a letter 9th.March 2017 from Mr. Frost (Woodfine's) dated 7th. March 2017. The letter was in response to my letter dated 25th. February 2017 in which Mr. Frost made a vague attempt to answer the questions in my letter.

I responded to Mr. Frost's letter dated 7th. March 2017 on 12th. March 2017.I set out my thoughts, regarding his evasive answers to various questions. I also informed him that because of ongoing investigations and because all evidence had been collated, I could see no useful purpose in a meeting; unless they had any positive thoughts on how to reconcile my concerns. I further informed him that I intend to pursue the matter through the Legal Ombudsman and other avenues. I stated that if they wished to respond to my letter, I would be prepared to listen to avoid any unpleasantness.

On 12th. March 2017 I also sent a letter to the Legal Ombudsman informing them of events and enclosed copies of correspondence between Woodfine's and myself. I also enclosed a very informative letter written by Mr. Connaughton to Dorset Police (CID) which made reference to my case.

I received a letter from Mr. Frost (Woodfine's) 23rd. March 2017. The letter was in response to my letter dated 12th. March 2017. At the end of the letter he states *"If we do not hear nothing by 10ᵗʰ. April 2017, we shall continue with proceedings in respect of our unpaid costs".*

Mr. Connaughton wrote a long response to Woodfine's 31ˢᵗ. March 2017, requesting answers to previous questions. I received an E.mail 4ᵗʰ. April 2017 from Mr. Frost regarding letter from Mr. Connaughton.... I responded to Mr. Frost's E.mail 5ᵗʰ. April 2017.

Dear Mr Frost,

THE BOWERS CASE

I have seen your letter ANF/SW/BO/083499-0001 dated 23 March 2017 and have been invited by Mr Bowers to comment.

Your Ms Sandbach had been an occasional legal representative on Mr Bowers' behalf. He arranged for her to intercede with the High Court in respect of the Planning Court Order dated 21 January 2016 with a date of service of 2 February 2016. The Judge had been misdirected in so far as she described his application for judicial review as 'an abuse of process'. He should, she said, have commenced with an application for statutory review. The Judge was wrong in law: Mr Bowers was correct. At Mr Bowers' behest, your Ms Sandbach conveyed that information to the Judge.

In her Order dated 9 May 2016, effective 12 May 2016, "after service of this order upon his solicitors" (Woodfines), the Judge's mea culpa agreed "this claim was correctly brought by way of a judicial review". Mr Bowers was granted 14 days in which to renew his application, that is, on or before 26 May 2016. Two important words had been overlooked by you and GLD - "costs reserved".

Mr Bowers spent the first week attempting to confirm he wanted Ms Sandbach to proceed and confirm to the Court his original intention to go to judicial review. He was assured on a daily basis that Ms Sandbach would return his calls but she never did. It is assumed she had already left the employment of Woodfines for her new post in Luton.

- When Keith Jones sought to achieve accommodation with HMCTS, the date was 26 May, the fourteenth day. In that email he said Woodfines had never put themselves on the Court record despite an exchange of letters between Woodfines and the Court. You admitted you had sent Mr Bowers a notice of acting in person for him to complete and return. Mr Bowers sent the document to the Court, copied to Woodfines, on 25 May 2016 but expressly declared he did not wish Woodfines to represent him. Why had you done this? You told HMCTS: "It would be an unnecessary breach of confidence to explain why at this stage"! You concluded your email to the High Court with the following ingratiating words: "If the court feels able to declare of its own

108

motion that we are not the claimant's solicitors on the record that would be very helpful in all the circumstances". It would avoid the embarrassment of explaining how and why you had missed the Judge's deadline.

Mr Bowers' assessment was that if he were to delay any longer from taking unilateral action, the opportunity would be lost; he had to take charge. Both HMCTS and the Parliamentary Ombudsman agree he set his intentions directly before HMCTS in an email they received on 24 May - the twelfth day. The Administrative Court Office's email to your Catherine Sandbach dated 26 May 2016 reminded the solicitors Mr Bowers' correspondence in future should be sent via his instructed representatives as opposed from him directly. HMCTS' Redgrave and GLD's John-Charles were found to have either wrongfully intervened or failed to intervene in the due process. There was a colleague, an Inspector, to protect from appearance before a Judicial Review.

Permit me now to return to the opening sentence: "We cannot ask the court to waive a fee which is legally payable because you disagree with a judge". How can a fee arise in a case where the Judge admits it was she who was at fault? In what manner did Mr Bowers disagree with the Judge? I suspect you are not an fait with the nuances of this case.

It is unwise to threaten members of the public. I have in mind the last sentence in the referenced letter: "If we hear nothing further by Monday 10 April 2017, we shall continue with the proceedings in respect of our unpaid costs". I seem to remember your claim for bogus costs was heard at Bedford County Court on 14 February 2017. I recall judgement being set aside, the writ cancelled and costs denied. There was also the revelation you had the impertinence to have a restriction order placed on Mr Bowers' property at the Land Registry. What do you think you are doing? You were representing an elderly man who has had his private property filched. Now we find his solicitor making a move on his home. You are invited to explain to Mr Bowers the nature and origin of your present "unpaid costs". Does your professional body support your behaviour?

I see here an absolute failure in your duty of care. To ignore a judge's provision, to have no one willing to receive clients' instructions, is not how civilised solicitors behave. If there had been someone available to receive and set down Mr Bowers' washes on your official paper, we are unlikely to have had the present problem with uncompliant public servants. Mr Bowers has been fighting his case for over 25 yeai-s, in which time he has lost his entire life savings. He relied upon you. You let him down. You can argue that you were not on the record. You provide your own corollary to such a status where the court deals with you as if you are, "and we fully appreciate that in many cases it is expedient and entirely proper to do so". The least you can do now is to contact the case progression official in the Administrative Court office, tell her what has happened and have this case restored to where it rightfully belongs.

Mr Bowers put down five questions for considered replies, together with a supplementary question:

- We had a 'no win, no fee arrangement'. How did the creative accounting figure of £7053.57 arise?
- What was the rationale for the involvement of Courts in Salford and Oldham?
- How do you account for your failure to support me?
- How do you propose to have a Judicial Review reinstated in the public interest and me compensated for the distress caused?
- Why did you find it necessary, unbeknown to me, to involve the Land Registry and my home?
- Are you familiar with the Mear case?
-

Yours sincerely,

Richard Connaughton

....

I received a discharge Order 7th. April 2017 from Salford Court (Dep. Judge Thexton) dated 6th. April 2017.

I received an E.mail from Woodfine's 13th. April 2017 attaching a statement of accounts. They are still reluctant to answer any questions. I agreed to a meeting with them.

I received an E.mail from Woodfine's 18th. April 2017 stating that, because I had referred my case to the Legal Ombudsman, they assumed I did not wish to meet with them. I responded stating that I am still prepared to meet with them subject to the conditions I had previously stated.

I received a phone call at 3.45pm 26th. April 2017 from Susan Parton (Legal Ombudsman). She informed me that she had been assigned to investigate my case CMP046872. NOTE: I informed her that I intended to inform the Newspapers about my dealings with Woodfine,s. She advised me not to contact newspapers until investigations had taken place. I received a letter from Susan Parton (Legal Ombudsman) 27th. April 2017. She requested further information which should be provided by 17th. May 2017.

NOTE!
Because of the complexity of my case, I had to refer to my very extensive file to prepare a summary of events to be considered by the Legal Ombudsman.

I wrote to Susan Parton 1st. May 2017 and enclosed an extensive file regarding Woodfine,s.

I wrote to Susan Parton again 20th. May 2017 and enclosed a letter written to Woodfine.s by Mr. Richard Connaughton. I also enclosed a letter I had written to Parliamentary Ombudsman concerning my experience while attending the Royal Courts of Justice. (RCJ), The reason for my visiting the RCJ. was a direct result of the incompetence and maladministration of Woodfine,s. Because of the actions/non-actions of Woodfine,s I had been subjected too much distress and financial burden over the past year.

I received an E.mail from Susan Parton 10th. July 2017 informing me that she had received information from Woodfine;s and is currently finalising her preliminary decision and hoped to inform me within next two weeks,

I received a letter from Susan Parton dated 21st. July 2017 giving her Preliminary Decision on Case: CMP-046872. Regarding Woodfine;s (Solicitors). It was in the usual negative form one expects from Ombudsman.

I received a message from Susan Parton 31st. July 2017 requesting a response to her E.mail dated 21st July 2017..I responded 1st. August 2017.

I sent a letter to Susan Parton dated 4th. August 2017 stating that I did not accept her decision sent 21st. July 2017 and giving reasons why, and enclosing various documents to support my feelings.

I received a response from Susan Parton 7th. August 2017 stating, she had passed my comments onto the Ombudsman, and I should hear within ten weeks,

I sent a copy of a document called "J'accuse II" and covering letter to Susan Parton, 14th. August 2017. The document is an informative and accurate report of the Malfeasance within certain bodies while I was trying to obtain "Justice". She responded 29th. August 2017 acknowledging receipt of documents.

I sent a letter to Susan Parton 19th. November 2017 informing her of much opposition I had received from various bodies in an attempt to pervert the Course of Justice. In the form of Lies and Maladministration in an attempt to prevent me obtaining "Justice". I received an acknowledgement to my letter 23rd. November 2017

I sent an E.mail to Susan Parton 16th. January 2018 and left voicemail requesting an update on my Case: CMP-046872. I received a response later that day informing me that I should have a decision within next 4 weeks.

I received an E.mail from Jason Chapman (Legal Ombudsman) 1st. February 2017 informing me that he had seen the report sent to me by Susan Parton. He states *"I have come to a significantly different conclusion from the one set out in the report". I therefore want to give you and the service provider an opportunity to comment on the attached provisional decision before it becomes final". Please respond in writing by 15th. February 2018 with any comments on this provisional decision"*

I received an E.mail from Susan Parton 7th. February 2018 reminding me to respond by 15th. February 2018. I responded 8th. February 2018 stating that I had drafted a response and would send the final copy by recorded delivery within 2 days.

I sent my lengthy response to Jason Chapman (Legal Ombudsman) 8th. February 2018 (sent recorded delivery).

I received an E.mail from Susan Parton 15th February 2018 acknowledging my letter dated 8th. February 2018. She states that because I do not accept the Ombudsman Provisional Decision the case had been passed back to the Ombudsman for consideration, and it is hoped to be finalised within the next 10 weeks.

I received an E.mail. from Jason Chapman 28th, March 2018 with an attached letter dated 27th. March 2018. The letter was 5 pages long. It basically stated that the service I had received from Woodfine's failed to provide a reasonable level of service and identified specified items of the service/non-service they provided. They did not consider the actions of Woodfine's regarding the Court Hearing "Shortest Court Hearing". To be wrong. They state *"I note and accept that this happened, but, I do not consider this to be material to the complaints by Mr. Bowers".* The letter also states that *" I am not persuaded, as Mr. Bowers has claimed, that the fact that the Judge set the order aside, or that they wrote to the Administrative Court in what Mr. Bowers has described as "Grovelling Communication" is proof that the firm failed to provide duty of care to him during the period that they acted or that there was misconduct on their part"......* It should be noted. The Judge made his decision because, Woodfine's attended the court earlier and withdrew they claim.

It is said that Ombudsman are "Like Tigers without teeth". I must agree, that is a fair description of my dealings with all Ombudsman I have had the misfortune to deal with.

I E.mailed Mr. Chapman (Legal Ombudsman) 4th. April 2018 explaining that I had recently moved house and had been without telephone and internet for 2 weeks; and would respond to his letter as soon as possible.

I received an E.mail from Legal Ombudsman 9th April 2018 stating I had one day to respond to their request 28/3/2018.

I responded the same day explaining that I had not had a response to my E.mail dated 4th April 2018; and stated I disputed the Ombudsman's report, and would respond as soon as possible,

I sent a letter to Mr. Chapman (Legal Ombudsman) 12th. April 2018. (special delivery). I gave my reasons for disputing the decision they had made.

I sent an E.mail to Mr. Chapman 30th. April 2018 requesting a response to my letter dated 12th. April 2018.

I received an E.mail from Bride Scully (General Enquires Team Legal Ombudsman) 14:19 1st. May 2018 stating " *Mr. Chapman has now considered your comments but has nothing to add to his final decision" She also added "Please let us know in writing, by the close of business today (midnight) whether you accept or reject it. We will then have to close the matter as an assumed rejection, if we do not hear from you"*

NOTE! They sometimes take 10 weeks to respond; and they want me to respond in writing, within 9 hours.

I phoned Ms. Scully immediately. She was very pleasant but had been instructed by Mr. Chapman. Who, had neither the will or courage to inform me himself?

I sent an Email to Ms. Scully 1st. May 2018 stating: *Thank you for your patience in talking to me on the phone this afternoon. You were very pleasant, but unfortunately you have to deliver messages which Mr. Chapman has neither the will or the courage to carry out himself. I totally reject his decision regarding the actions of Woodfine Solicitors. I realise this is the outcome you have always required. However, I will pursue by other means".*

CONCLUSION:

Ombudsman are there to be seen to distribute "Justice". However, they are very cautious and well skilled in ensuring that certain Authorities, Business's and prominent people are not exposed for the wrong's they do.

FOOTNOTE:

It is hoped that some courageous and honest person is prepared to place their head above the parapet and investigate the obvious Malfeasance within parts of our society. Alan Bowers.

E.mail: bowers-alan@sky.com

CHAPTER II

A BRIEFING OF THE ACTIONS AND CONDUCT OF
CATHERINE ANN SANDBACH (SOLICITOR)
AND HER EMPLOYER WOODFINES
SOLICITOR (BEDFORD)
JULY 2014 – MAY 2016.

It has been discovered by investigation; that, the service and treatment of Mr. Alan Bowers by WOODFINES SOLICITORS 0BEDFORD) during the period July 2014- May 2016 was unacceptable and unprofessional.

It has also been revealed that other clients of WOODFINES SOLICITOR (BEDFORD) also received similar service/treatment during the same period. The Solicitor involved was CATHERINE ANN SANDBACH and Senior partner Mr. KEITH JONES.

Although their conduct was reported to The Legal Ombudsman and much evidence was supplied over a long period, it resulted in an ambiguous and bias decision. The Ombudsman agreed Mr. Bowers had been poorly treated. After sometime The Legal Ombudsman gave an unacceptable decision, and stated they would not pursue the case further and would not accept any further discussion regarding the matter.

It has been revealed that action was taken by "Solicitors Disciplinary Tribunal" concerning some clients of WOODFINES SOLICITORS (BEDFORD).

The result of the action taken resulted in CATHERINE ANN SANDBACH being "Struck of the Roll" and fined £2600 costs.

This document reveals and indicates the wrong doings and unacceptable treatment supplied by WOODFINES SOLICITORS (BEDFORD).

NOTE! Details and Transcript of "Solicitors Disciplinary Tribunal" are also available in my files.

Dishonest solicitor misled clients about case progress to 'buy time'

By John Hyde | 12 February 2020

 solicitor who repeatedly misled clients - claiming she wanted to buy herself time to deal with a busy workload – has been struck off the roll.

Catherine Sandbach was found to have told 'mistruths' on three separate matters to conceal her own inaction, providing them with false reassurances about progress on their cases.

Sandbach, admitted in 2009, had already said she was leaving the profession for good, and she was banned by the Solicitors Disciplinary Tribunal following a regulatory settlement agreement between herself and the SRA.

The tribunal heard that Sandbach admitted dishonesty in relation to all three matters. She told one client a boundary dispute was progressing through the court when she knew court proceedings had not been issued. She did the same – this time over a period of nine months – with a client in a business dispute matter. Sandbach also acted for a client on an annulment of a bankruptcy order and admitted fabricating and backdating an email purportedly sent to the Insolvency Service in order to mislead him into believing she had acted on his instructions.

Sandbach's misconduct took place while she was a solicitor in the litigation department in the Bedford office of Woodfines Solicitors. She was dismissed in 2016.

In mitigation, which was not endorsed by the SRA, Sandbach said she was under a great deal of stress and claimed to have a 'significant' workload, with limited resources offered by her employer. She said she was expected by the firm to deal with matters beyond her experience as a solicitor, which exacerbated her stress. She produced a medical report saying her conduct was influenced by work-related stress which brought on symptoms of anxiety and depression. She was sorry for the difficulties faced by clients as a result of her behaviour and made no personal gain from what she did, claiming her actions were 'simply to buy herself more time to deal with her ever-increasing workload'.

117

SOLICITORS DISCIPLINARY TRIBUNAL

IN THE MATTER OF THE SOLICITORS ACT 1974   Case No. 12016-2019

BETWEEN:

SOLICITORS REGULATION AUTHORITY   Applicant

and

CATHERINE ANN SANDBACH   Respondent

Before:

Mr J. A. Astle (in the chair)
Mr W. Ellerton
Mrs S. Gordon

Date of Hearing: 14 January 2020

Appearances

There were no appearances as the matter was dealt with on the papers.

JUDGMENT ON AN AGREED OUTCOME

Allegations

1.   The Allegations against the Respondent, a solicitor and formerly an assistant solicitor in the litigation department at Woodfines Solicitors LLP ("the firm"), made by the Applicant were that she:

1.1   Between 1 February 2016 and 31 May 2016, deliberately misled her client Ms SD in relation to her boundary dispute matter by causing Ms SD to believe that her matter was progressing through the Court when she knew that Court proceedings had not been issued, thereby breaching all or alternatively any of Principles 2, 4, 5 and 6 of the SRA Principles 2011 and failing to achieve Outcomes 1.1 and 1.5 of the SRA Code of Conduct 2011.

1.2   Between 1 August 2015 and 31 May 2016, deliberately misled her client Mr TM in relation to his business dispute matter by causing Mr TM to believe that his matter was progressing through the Court when she knew that Court proceedings had not been issued, thereby breaching all or alternatively any of Principles 2, 4, 5 and 6 of the SRA Principles 2011 and failing to achieve Outcomes 1.1 and 1.5 of the SRA Code of Conduct 2011.

1.3   On or around 14 December 2015, whilst acting for Mr SJ on an annulment of a bankruptcy order matter, fabricated and backdated an e-mail (dated 30 November 2015 and timed at 15:12) purportedly sent to the Insolvency Service in order to mislead her client Mr SJ into believing that she had acted on his instructions and issued the annulment application by the 30 November 2015 deadline when she knew that was not true as she had not issued the annulment application, thereby breaching all or alternatively any of Principles 2, 4, 5 and 6 of the SRA Principles 2011 and failing to achieve Outcomes 1.1, 1.2 and 1.5 of the SRA Code of Conduct 2011.

In addition, Allegations 1.1, 1.2 and 1.3 inclusive were advanced on the basis that the Respondent's conduct was dishonest. Dishonesty was alleged as an aggravating feature of the Respondent's misconduct but was not an essential ingredient in proving the Allegations.

Factual Background

2.   The Respondent was admitted to the Roll of Solicitors on 15 September 2009. At the time of the Rule 5 statement the Respondent did not hold a current practising certificate. At the material time she was working as an assistant solicitor in the litigation department at the firm, the address of which is: 16 St Cuthbert's Street, Bedford, MK40 3JG.

Application for the matter to be resolved by way of Agreed Outcome

3.   The parties invited the Tribunal to deal with the Allegations against the Respondent in accordance with the Statement of Agreed Facts and Outcome dated 10 January 2020 annexed to this Judgment ("the Agreed Outcome"). The parties submitted that the outcome proposed was consistent with the Tribunal's Guidance Note on Sanctions.

4.   In the Agreed Outcome the Respondent admitted all the Allegations against her including the allegation of dishonesty. The agreed sanction was that she be struck-off the Roll and it was further agreed that she pay costs in the sum of £2,600.

Findings of Fact and Law

5.   The Applicant was required to prove the allegations beyond reasonable doubt. The Tribunal had due regard to the Respondent's rights to a fair trial and to respect for her private and family life under Articles 6 and 8 of the European Convention for the Protection of Human Rights and Fundamental Freedoms.

6.   The Tribunal reviewed all the material before it and was satisfied beyond reasonable doubt that the Respondent's admissions were properly made.

7.   The Tribunal considered the Guidance Note on Sanction (November 2019). In doing so the Tribunal assessed the culpability and harm identified together with the aggravating and mitigating factors that existed.

8.   The Tribunal noted that this was a case involving significant dishonesty. It was repeated across several clients over a period of time. The Tribunal agreed that the appropriate sanction was a strike-off on the basis that no lesser sanction was justified given the severity of the misconduct. The Tribunal then considered whether there were any exceptional circumstances such that would justify a lesser sanction than a strike-off. There were no such circumstances advanced and the Tribunal did not identify any based on the material before it. It was a sad case but one that could only result in the Respondent being struck-off the Roll. The Tribunal therefore approved the Agreed Outcome.

Costs

9.   The Tribunal was content with the level of costs agreed between the parties.

Statement of Full Order

10.   The Tribunal Ordered that the Respondent, CATHERINE ANN SANDBACH, solicitor, be STRUCK OFF the Roll of Solicitors and it further Ordered that she do pay the costs of and incidental to this application and enquiry fixed in the sum of £2,600.00.

Dated this 23rd day of January 2020
On behalf of the Tribunal

J. A. Astle
Chairman

CHAPTER: III

MY STRUGGLE FOR JUSTICE
"THE PATH AND I" CONTINUED

After my rejection by "The Legal Ombudsman" 1st. May 2018 regarding investigating the conduct of Woodfines Solicitors I felt defeated in my attempts to obtain "JUSTICE"

However, during the month of February 2020 while searching the internet I discovered very interesting information concerning Woodfines Solicitors (Bedford)

I discovered other clients of Woodfines had also experienced misconduct regarding their dealings with Woodfines at the same time that Woodfines had been acting for me. Three former clients had reported their experiences to "Solicitors Regulation Authority".

The actions of Woodfines had been placed before "Solicitors Disciplinary Tribunal" 14th.January 2020. The findings of the Tribunal resulted in Ms. Catherine Ann Sandbach being "STRUCK OF THE ROLLS" for misconduct and dishonesty.

Catherine Ann Sandbach (Solicitor 431024) was the same solicitor who acted for me from August 2015-May 2016. It was also discovered that Catherine Ann Sandbach was an assistant solicitor under the guidance of Mr. Keith Jones, a senior partner at Woodfines.

I made a request to "Legal Ombudsman" (28th. September 2016.) to investigate the actions and conduct of Woodfines. I supplied many documents and statements to the "Legal Ombudsman". After many months, the Ombudsman stated. I had been poorly treated by Woodfines but they could find no evidence of Misconduct.

On investigating further, I obtained details of "Solicitors Regulation Authority" submission to Solicitors Disciplinary Tribunal dated 14th. January 2020 and the outcome of the proceedings. I also obtained a copy of an article which appeared in the "Law Society Gazette" regarding the dishonesty of Catherine Ann Sandbach.

I also obtained a copy of the whole proceedings of the case submitted to the "Solicitors Disciplinary Tribunal" which included statements by Mr. Keith Jones and other employees of Woodfines.

Having discovered this information I produced a document called "Justice what Justice" including a report upon "Catherine Ann Sandbach and Mr. Keith Jones a partner in Woodfines Solicitors (Bedford).

In view of this newly found evidence, I wrote to the "Legal Ombudsman" 18th. March 2020 asking them to review my case. The letter was sent recorded delivery, I also enclosed two documents "Justice what Justice" and a report concerning Catherine Ann Sandbach (Solicitor 431024). I also wrote to Sarah Craddock (Legal secretary) Woodfines, informing her of my actions and requested that all the evidence I had supplied be returned to me.

Having had no acknowledgement or response from Legal Ombudsman, I telephoned them 2nd. April 2020 at 9.27am and spoke to a lady called Ron. I also sent E.mail

Details of E.mail & call

Complaint

From: Alan Bowers (bowers-alan@sky.com)

To: inquires@legalombudsman.org.uk

Date: Thursday, 2 April 2020, 09:42 BST

To whom it may concern.
I wrote to the Legal Ombudsman 18th. March 2010 regarding an old complaint No,CMP-046872, I also enclosed 2 documents for your informaion. Because I have not received any acknowledgement or response, I telephoned you 9.27am. 2nd. April 2020 and spoke to a lady called Ron. She informed me that my request had been received and I should have a response within 4 weeks. She also informed me that if I sent in by Email. I would have an immediate response. Therefore I would be grateful fo any information. I reaise these are very difficult times, however, please acknowledge my request.
Please see attached copy of my letter dated 18th. March 2020.
Regards
Alan Bowers

I also telephoned WOODFINES 9.27am. 2nd. April 2020 and requested to speak with Sarah Craddock and was informed she was working from home and I should send her an E.mail.

I received a letter by E.mail 2nd. April from Andrew Carter (Milton Keynes office). The E.mail stated that the complaint had been determined by the "Legal Ombudsman" and they have no obligation to comment further. The letter also informed me that they will continue to retain all my documents, see copy of letter

Our Ref: AXC/CH/BO/083499-001
2 April 2020

By Email Only: bowers-alan@sky.com

Dear Mr Bowers

I refer to your letter dated 20 March 2020 to Sarah Craddock at our Bedford office.

Your complaint has been determined by the Legal Ombudsman and we have no obligation to comment any further.

As we have explained previously, and I refer to Mr Jones' letter dated 27 September 2018, we will not send you any papers or allow you to collect them (which in any event is prohibited at this time owing to the COVID-19 crisis) because there are still costs outstanding in respect of our involvement in your case. We therefore continue to retain a lien over your papers.

Yours sincerely

Andrew Carter

Andrew Carter
(email: acarter@woodfines.co.uk)

The 6th. April 2020 , I sent a letter and copy of "Justice what Justice" to Andrew Carter
(Woodfine Milton Keynes Office). The package was sent Recorded Delivery.
I also informed Sarah Craddock (Bedford).
The letter and document was received and signed for by Woodfines Milton Keynes at 9.7am. 7th. April 2020.

I received a letter from Legal Ombudsman dated 6th. April 2020 (no indication who the letter was from and no signiture). The letter was in its usual negative form stating that all the new information I had sent to them 18th. March 2020 was not related to my case and they will not be re-opening my case. I telephoned the Legal Ombudsman immediately I received the letter. and was informed there is nothing they could do.
   I sent another letter and a document called "My struggle tp obtain Jusice" by recorded delivery on Saturday 11th. April 2020 (see copy of letter below) It was posted and recorded at Flitwick Post office at 11.46am Reference No. NV072765860GB.

Your Ref. F077238/ CMP-046872

Dear Sir/Madam

Thank you for your letter dated 6th. April 2020. Your letter did not indicate who the letter was from, and had no signature.

The contents of your letter were disappointing but not surprising, I have been dealing with Ombudsman for many years and have discovered they do not tell lies, they just do not tell the truth.

The evidence I have provided to you in the Document "Justice what Justice" which includes details of action taken against Woodfines Solicitors, in general and Ms. Catherine Ann Sandbach and Mr. Keith Jones in particular, cannot be denied.

In your letter to me dated 27th. March 2020 (Copy enclosed) you state (Para.11)
   "it would be for other clients of the firm to raise complaints if they felt that the firm had provided them with poor service". You now have proof of Woodfines poor service, including Lies, Deceit, and Dishonesty at the same time the company was acting for me. This proof is in the form of action taken against them by "Solicitors Regulation Authority" and "Solicitors Disciplinary Tribunal"

However, in typical fashion you have pushed this evidence aside and continue to state Woodfines "as a firm" are not liable for any misconduct. The evidence you have is COGENT and UNDENIABLE.

I therefore hope you will reconsider your position, and act in accordance with the function of your purpose. "Justice being seen to be done".

I have enclosed copies of letters and documents for your consideration.

Yours faithfully,
Alan Bowers.

Enclosed letters: Dated 27th. March 2018, 8th. February 2018, 12th. April 2018,
Document: "My Struggle for Justice"

Sent recorded delivery

I tried to track the delivery Thursdy 16th. April 2020 but it only revealed that letter was received at Flitwick Post office... no further details. I contacted Legal Ombudsman 9.30am Thursday 16th. April 2020 and was advised that they had not received the documents and was advised to call back Monday 20th. April.

Documents delivered to Legal Ombudsman 4.44am 17th. April 20120 signed by EDM/JOHN

I received a photo-copy response from Ombudsman dated 29th. April 2020. No name or signature.

Usual negative response, stating; *" Thank you for you letter dated 9th. April 2020. As stated in our letter to you dated 6th. April 2020, we are unable to consider your complaint. any further and we will not be re-opening your case.*
Any further letters will be read and placed on file but may not be responded to.
You may wish to consider seeking independent legal advice and taking your own legal advice going forward".

As usual it is their policy; if you do not respond, the problem will go away.

Having had no comunications from Legal Ombudsman or Woodfines, I decided to write to both 13th. May 2020.
Details are illustrated below.

Your Ref. AXC/CH/BO/083499-001

Dear Mr. Carter

As you have not responded to my letter dated 6th. April 2020 I am assuming that you believe if one ignores an issue it will hopefully go away.

I wish to advise you, that I and others are pursuing the issue and it will NOT go away, and we are in the process of revealing much that is corrupt and improper within various Departments and other Institutions such as yourselves.

You have the opportunity of responding to my requests or totally ignoring them as you have indicated.

We are all living in desperate and worrying times at the moment. I therefore, urge you to consider your, and your companies' situation, in failing to carry out your duty of care.

Keep safe.
Yours faithfully,

Alan Bowers (Sent special delivery)

Over the next few weeks, I exchanged letters with Legal Ombudsman and Woodfines (Solicitors). Most responses from both were negative and non-sensical. Eventually, I received a letter from Woodfines in which it states. *"I am not concerned or aggrieved by your publication: it is a catalogue of events and subjective opinions which exposes the fulmination of a former client of Woodfines who is at odds with the judicial system because he was unable to prosecute a plausible claim for misconduct in public office."*

NOTE! This is not impression given by the tone of their letter dated 26th. June.

The letter also states. *"Whilst you may continue to be disgruntled about a legal remedy which was never within your legitimate grasp, this is your own business and it not something which will occupy the minds of this firm or its members any further. This is the final response you will receive from us. Any further correspondence from you will not be responded to and will be placed directly onto your archived file".*

Note! Error "and it not something". I am so glad Woodfines no longer act for me!

Woodfines opinion of the strength of my case seems to changed. Initially they informed me that my case had been considered by their Litigation team and they considered my case to be strong enough for them to enter into a "Conditional Fee Agreement" (CFA).

The agreement was signed by myself and Woodfines, 10th. November 2014.

CONCLUSION:

The contents of this document reveal the corruption and maleficence within certain sections of Government Departments and other institutions, throughout the land.

Most of us accept corruption, and unacceptable behaviour exists in many parts of the world, but, we do not expect to experience it in our own country.

It has been said "All that is needed for evil to triumph is for good men and women to do nothing". However, we find many law-abiding citizens are subjected to distress and financial burden; because of the actions of a few who appear to derive pleasure out of causing distress to others.

It can be seen from the contents of this document that many Authorities and Organisations are prepared to use any means such as. (Lies, deceit, false statements, destroying of documents) to prevent them from being called to account for their wrong doings. And, thereby avoiding any repercussions, such as; failure, reputational risks, costs of compensation due.

When an ordinary citizen attempts to challenge the "Establishment" (Government, Local Authorities etc.) they face resistance, by those who do not wish to be exposed for their wrong doings. Their strategy is to ignore the issue or by imposing costs; by ignoring the issue they hope the problem will go away.

They know most people cannot afford to employ Lawyers, Solicitors etc. to fight their case, and rely upon this to deter them from pursuing their "Struggle for Justice", and thereby avoiding risk of having to pay compensation for the distress they have caused.

As the Legal Ombudsman works with the Ministry of Justice, it can be assumed that it works with the Government and safe guards its interest.

Through my investigations I have found that it would have been better to have sought Justice through the "Solicitors Regulation Authority" who should be independent of Government influence. However, I chose to approach the "Legal Ombudsman" who do not appear to be independent.

Life is a learning curve, and we all learn through our mistakes.

Over the past 29 years I and my family have endured much distress and financial burden; and many have said **"Why do you not give up".** My answer is;

"because I was always taught to respect and accept JUSTICE". <u>**What Justice!**</u>

Lightning Source UK Ltd.
Milton Keynes UK
UKHW012305150321
380397UK00003B/41/J